The Dominion of Love

"Norm Phelps not only talks about the dominion of love, but embodies it in his everyday existence as well. By challenging the modern church's defense of the status quo regarding animal exploitation, it is books like *Dominion of Love* that will save the church from becoming, as Dr. Martin Luther King, Jr. forewarned, 'an irrelevant social club,' and instead place it where it belongs: at the forefront of the movement for social justice, standing in defense of the oppressed and downtrodden."—**Paul Shapiro**, Campaigns Manager, Compassion Over Killing

"The power of Norm Phelps's book comes from a combination of scholarly research and a deep understanding that love and compassion for all beings is the only foundation upon which a millennial world of peace and justice can be built."—**J. R. Hyland**, author, *God's Covenant with Animals*

"Grounded and ground-breaking, thoughtful and thought-provoking. Norm Phelps makes a compelling argument that the religious community should be leading—not inhibiting—the social movement for animal rights. This book is a necessary primer for animal advocates—believers and nonbelievers alike—who want to be persuasive in changing minds, hearts, and public policy."—**Michael Markarian**, Executive Vice President, The Fund for Animals

The Dominion of Love

Animal Rights According to the Bible

Norm Phelps

Lantern Books • New York
A Division of Booklight Inc.

2002
Lantern Books
One Union Square West, Suite 201
New York, NY 10003

Unless otherwise noted, all quotations from Scripture are taken
from the New American Standard Bible, Copyright 1960, 1962, 1963,
1968, 1971, 1972, 1973, 1975, 1977, 1995 by The Lockman Foundation.
Used by permission.

Several passages in this book have previously appeared in somewhat
different form in the booklet "Love for All Creatures: Frequently
Asked Questions about the Bible and Animal Rights," by Norm
Phelps, The Fund for Animals, New York, NY, 2001. Used by
permission.

Printed in the United States of America

Library of Congress Cataloging-in-Publication Data

Phelps, Norm.
  The dominion of love : animal rights according to the Bible / Norm
Phelps.
      p. cm.
Includes bibliographical references.
  ISBN 1-59056-009-4 (alk. paper)
  1. Animal welfare—Biblical teaching. 2. Animal rights—Biblical
teaching. 3. Animal welfare—Religious aspects—Christianity. 4.Animal
rights—Religious aspects—Christianity. I. Title.
  BS680.A5 P48 2002
  241'.693—dc21

                                              2002004105

You shall love your neighbor as yourself.
Leviticus 19:18

God is love, and the one who abides in love
abides in God, and God abides in him.
1 John 4:16

For the pigeons who died at Hegins—
and for Heidi, who never gave up.

Contents

Acknowledgments

First, a word of heartfelt appreciation to Martin Rowe of Lantern Books. His faith in *The Dominion of Love* and his wise editorial guidance, gently administered, made this book possible. Working with him is both a privilege and a pleasure.

Catherine Clyne, Walter Corrigan, Richard DeAngelis, Janice Fredericks, Sarah Gallogly, Jim Hoverman, Andea Lococo, Michael Markarian, Ginny Mead, Diana Norris, Peter Petersan, Heidi Prescott, Lewis Regenstein, Carrie Reulbach, Richard Robb, Patti Rogers, Paul Shapiro, Kim Stallwood, Barbara Stasz, and Vicki Stevens contributed ideas, comments, or encouragement that were instrumental to the completion of the manuscript in its final form. I thank them each and every one. Needless to say, responsibility for the views expressed and for any errors or misstatements is entirely mine.

I am extremely grateful for the unfailing support and encouragement of The Fund for Animals, where I work. The enthusiasm and confidence of President Marian Probst, Executive Vice President Michael Markarian, and National Director Heidi Prescott were invaluable to me throughout the ordeal that is writing a book.

Finally, I want to acknowledge three remarkable individuals who have touched my life in ways that led to this book.

Theresa Olson was my high school English teacher. An adherent of Albert Schweitzer's philosophy of reverence for life, she was the first ethical vegetarian I had ever met. In the frightened and narrow-minded world of the 1950s, hers was a lonely stand on behalf of openness and compassion, but she took that stand with courage and grace, and she persevered.

Patti Rogers lives the dominion of love to a degree that I can only admire and hope some day to approach. It was she who taught me the importance of loving all my neighbors, including those not of my species. Best friend, teacher, and partner, she encouraged, guided, and sustained me through the writing of this book.

Cleveland Amory, founder of The Fund for Animals, was a giant of the twentieth century. A best-selling author and popular television personality, from 1967 until his passing three decades later he devoted his life to defending the defenseless and, in a phrase he coined, "speaking for those who can't." Cleveland Amory found joy in life, and more than anything else, he wanted all who live to be able to know that same joy. There is nothing I say with more pride than, "Yes, I knew Cleveland Amory."

Norm Phelps

Introduction

I wrote *The Dominion of Love* to encourage all who revere the Bible as holy scripture to open their hearts to the suffering that we inflict upon our nonhuman neighbors. I approach this task in three ways. First, by showing that the right of animals not to be imprisoned, tortured, and killed for our benefit flows naturally from the Bible's message of love and compassion. Second, by examining the Bible's most important passages dealing with our relationship to animals. And finally, by responding to defenses of animal exploitation that are often made on the basis of the Bible.

Most chapters incorporate insights and perspectives from both Jewish and Christian authorities. The subjects we are discussing are not matters regarding which Jews and Christians find themselves on opposite sides of a theological fence. Animal rights may be an open topic of discussion within each tradition, but it is not a point of disagreement between the two traditions. On numerous occasions, I quote both Jewish and Christian commentators who use slightly different vocabularies to make very similar points. I hope that readers will find in the reading—as I did in the writing—that mother and daughter have much of value to share with one another. Both traditions are, after all, paths leading us to a common goal: learning to love God with all our hearts, souls, and strength, and to love our neighbors as ourselves.

*　*　*

The concept of rights, in the sense of "human rights," "women's rights," "animal rights," and the like is never mentioned in the Bible. It was created during the Enlightenment by philosophers looking for a way to ensure that those with power would treat those without power in accord, at least to some degree, with the Golden Rule. After 1,600 years of relying on individual conscience, the rich and powerful were still behaving as if the Golden Rule applied only to themselves and they were free to use and abuse everyone else as they saw fit. Something more was needed, some social mechanism that would apply the Golden Rule to everyone who needed its protection. That something more was the idea of human rights, enforceable by the state. In the two hundred plus years since the Enlightenment, we have made more progress in protecting the weak from the rapacity of the strong than had been made in all previous recorded history. Now, the same impulse that led Enlightenment philosophers to human rights is pointing us toward rights for the least powerful of those who live at the mercy of our society. We are living in the early years of an Enlightenment for the Animals. Individual conscience has failed to cast the protective mantle of the Golden Rule over animals just as it failed to cast it over humans. They, like us, need the implementing mechanism of rights.

No Jew or Christian today would argue that human rights ought to be abandoned because they are not explicitly taught in the Bible. Rather, Jews and Christians universally support human rights because they recognize them as essential to putting the Bible's ethical teachings to work in the world. Like human rights, animal rights can be understood as a response to the Bible's challenge to express the love and compassion of God in our lives as well as our liturgy.

* * *

Animals—at the very least, the more complex animals—are sentient beings. They have the same physical senses that we have, a central nervous system similar to ours, and brains that are highly developed in the areas that process physical and emotional sensation. They experience pleasure and pain, joy and suffering, in much the same ways that we do. No one who has shared his or her life with a dog, a cat, or a bird can doubt this. They may not speak our language—although they certainly understand it better than we understand theirs—but with a clarity that cannot be misunderstood, our companions express happiness, fear, anger, love, jealousy, anticipation, and all of the other emotions that we experience in ourselves.

Some will protest that this is "anthropomorphism," attributing human characteristics to nonhuman animals, but it is not. If I said that deer understand contract law or that robins can do calculus, that would be anthropomorphism. But when we attribute to nonhuman animals the physical and emotional sensations that they are physiologically equipped to experience, and of which their behavior gives constant evidence, we are simply acknowledging a fact.

As sentient beings, animals can suffer from our cruelty and benefit from our kindness. The Bible teaches kindness and condemns cruelty. It doesn't take a scholar or a theologian to draw the obvious conclusion.

A Note about Bibles and Reference Works
Unless otherwise indicated in the text, all quotations from the Bible are taken from the *New American Standard Bible, Updated*

Edition (NASB). Produced by Protestant scholars, the NASB is what Biblical specialists call a "verbal" or "formal equivalence" translation, that is, it attempts to translate the words of the ancient language directly into English without interpreting or paraphrasing them. What you read in the NASB replicates very closely what the ancient authors actually wrote, rather than what modern translators think they probably meant. In the jargon of Biblical scholarship, translations that try to interpret the authors' meaning for the reader rather than reproduce their actual words are sometimes called "dynamic equivalence" translations. For purposes of study, as opposed to worship or devotion, they can be misleading because the doctrinal biases of the translator affect the translation in ways that the reader cannot detect.

Alternate choices for Bibles that reflect what the ancient authors actually said—instead of interpreting their words according to what the translators think they must have meant—would include, for the Hebrew Scriptures, *Tanakh: The Holy Scriptures* (THS); and for both the Hebrew Scriptures and the New Testament, *The New American Bible* (NAB). Like the NASB, both are generally free from doctrinal bias. Being produced for Jewish and Catholic audiences, respectively, they include the Apocrypha, which the Protestant NASB does not.

In recent years, the *New International Version* (NIV) has become the best-selling Bible in the English-speaking world, displacing the King James Version after nearly four centuries of unchallenged supremacy, thanks in large part to a literary style that is fluid, natural, and contemporary. Closer to being a dynamic equivalence translation than the three versions recommended above (hence the superior literary quality of its prose), the NIV sometimes reflects the fundamentalist Protestant theology of its translators.

As for the King James Version (KJV), it is a verbal translation, and if you speak English as it was spoken in 1611 it can serve reasonably well. But the archaic language, while incomparably beautiful, presents severe problems. To cite one example that is particularly important to our subject, when the KJV was produced, "meat" meant any substantial food, whether of animal or vegetable origin. Accordingly, the KJV uses "meat" to translate fifteen Hebrew or Aramaic words and eight Greek words, several of which refer to food generally rather than specifically to the flesh of an animal.[1] The "meat offering" that is frequently mentioned in the KJV, for example, was actually a grain offering, which is what most modern translations call it.[2] Unsurpassed for devotion and liturgy, the KJV is not the best choice for Bible study.

* * *

The bulk of the Hebrew Scriptures are written in Hebrew and the remainder in Aramaic, a closely related language. The New Testament is written in Greek. In order that readers will not be tempted to suspect that I may have substituted wishful thinking for scholarship in these languages, I have relied upon reference works produced by conservative Christian authorities.[3] Most, including Strong's Exhaustive Concordance of the Bible, The Thayer Greek-English Lexicon of the New Testament, and The Brown, Driver, Briggs Hebrew and English Lexicon, have been used in colleges, seminaries, and churches for nearly a century or longer. On those rare occasions when I disagree with these authorities, I explain my reasons so that the reader can understand and evaluate them.

I have tried to keep the intrusion of Hebrew and Greek words to an absolute minimum, but it has not been possible to keep them out of the text entirely. Where I have had to include a Hebrew or Greek word or phrase, I have provided the Strong number in a footnote to make things easier for the reader who wants to research the word further. *Strong's Exhaustive Concordance of the Bible* assigns to each Hebrew, Aramaic, and Greek word that appears in the Bible a unique number. Readers can look up the English word (from the KJV), find the number of the Hebrew, Aramaic, or Greek word that it translates, and look up that word in the dictionary at the back of the *Concordance*. Other Biblical dictionaries and reference works are also often keyed to the Strong numbers. Since an English word may translate several Hebrew or Greek words, and the same Hebrew or Greek word may be translated by several English words, the Strong numbers can be a valuable tool.

There are, of course, concordances created for other translations, including the excellent *Zondervan NASB Exhaustive Concordance*, but their numbering systems are usually based on Strong's—if not identical to it—and the Strong numbers are so widely known and referenced that they seemed a natural choice.

A Note about Dates

In keeping with a practice increasingly followed by historians writing about this period, I have used BCE (Before the Common Era) in place of the more familiar BC, and CE (Common Era) in place of AD. 100 BCE equals 100 BC, while 100 CE is the same as AD 100.

Notes

1. Strong, "Meat," pp. 899–900.
2. This offering is described in Leviticus 2:1–16 and 6:14–18.
3. These are listed in the Bibliography under Bibles and Bible Study Aids.

1: An Eternal Treblinka

A nimals live at the mercy of humankind. We can treat them however we like without fear of repercussions. Our power is as close to absolute as power can be, and the fate they suffer at our hands demonstrates the wisdom of the Catholic historian Lord Acton, who said, "Power tends to corrupt, and absolute power corrupts absolutely."[1] Our power over animals is so total and universal that we are hardly aware of it. Daily we sacrifice their lives to our convenience with hardly a second thought.

Every year in the United States alone:

- Ten million dogs and cats, normal, healthy, ready to share love and companionship, are put to death because the available homes are overwhelmed by the sheer number of animals who need homes.[2]
- More than 20 million animals—including mice, rats, guinea pigs, rabbits, cats, dogs, monkeys, and great apes—are imprisoned and killed in biomedical and product testing laboratories.[3]
- One-hundred-thirty-five million animals who live in the wild—including 17 million ducks, 27 million squirrels, and 35 million mourning doves—are killed for amusement by hunters.[4]

- Ten billion farmed animals, including 9 billion chickens, are killed after short lives spent in prison-like conditions of intensive confinement because we enjoy the taste of their flesh.[5]

Looking at our treatment of animals, the great twentieth-century Yiddish writer and winner of the Nobel Prize for Literature, Isaac Bashevis Singer, wrote of "all those scholars, all those philosophers, all the leaders of the world" who "have convinced themselves that man, the worst transgressor of all the species, is the crown of creation. All other creatures were created merely to provide him with food, pelts, to be tormented, exterminated. In relation to them, all people are Nazis; for the animals, it is an eternal Treblinka. And yet man demands compassion from heaven."[6]

Elsewhere, Singer expressed the view that all violence is interconnected. ". . . As long as human beings will go on shedding the blood of animals, there will never be any peace," he said in the forward to a book on vegetarianism. "There is only one little step from killing animals to creating gas chambers à la Hitler and concentration camps à la Stalin . . . There will be no justice as long as man will stand with a knife or with a gun and destroy those who are weaker than he is."[7] This was written by a man who lost his mother and a brother to the death camps, who barely escaped Nazi Europe himself. He understood that all injustice, oppression, and cruelty flow from the same source: the notion that some groups are inherently entitled to our compassion and kindness, while others are not. Once that basic principle is accepted, it is an easy thing to create new classes of victims simply by pushing them outside our perimeter of protection.[8]

As a child, Dr. Alex Hershaft, founder and president of the Farm Animal Reform Movement (FARM), survived the destruction of the Warsaw ghetto by the Nazis. Addressing the national conference that FARM hosts every year, Dr. Hershaft recently said, "In the Warsaw ghetto, I learned that human beings can treat other human beings like animals. From that, I concluded that the only way to end all oppression is to eliminate the oppression of the most oppressed—nonhuman animals."[9]

Christian theologian and humanitarian Albert Schweitzer expressed an understanding similar to Singer's and Hershaft's when he said, "Until he extends the circle of his compassion to all living things, man will not himself find peace."[10]

In the last decade of his life, Albert Schweitzer put this principle into practice by becoming a vegetarian. Isaac Bashevis Singer was a lifelong vegetarian, as is Alex Hershaft. By refusing to eat the flesh of slaughtered animals, all three have acknowledged what most of us refuse to admit. The responsibility for this global system of concentration camps and killing floors does not rest solely with those who personally imprison, torture, and kill the victims. It sits upon the shoulders of every one of us who agrees to benefit from it. Every time we go into a supermarket and come out with a package of lamb chops, every time we go into a diner and order scrambled eggs and bacon, we become just as responsible for the suffering and death of the lamb, the chicken, or the pig as if we had wielded the bloody knife ourselves. The innocent animal was killed to satisfy our appetite. *If no one bought the meat, the milk, and the eggs, no one would imprison and kill the animals.* In the same way, every time we buy a dog or cat from a pet shop or a breeder, every time we allow our companion animals to have babies, we become responsible for the death of an animal who is executed because we bought or bred instead of going to a shelter and taking home a new friend whose life depended on our thoughtfulness. They are waiting for us there in the shelters. They are counting on us for their lives, and we fail them because we insist on made-to-order. They are dying of our selfishness.

Human use of animals is the most widespread and oppressive system of abuse and extermination that has ever existed, and all who enjoy the products are responsible for the process. However hard we may try, we can no more absolve ourselves from responsibility by refusing to think about it than we can escape an onrushing train by turning our back to it. Reality is real whether we look the other way or not. So is responsibility.

*   *   *

I say "responsibility" rather than "guilt," because in most cases it is not a question of individuals deliberately committing acts they know to be wrong, but something more subtle, more pervasive, and harder to change. The vast majority of those responsible for the abuse and killing of animals are good people who are trying to live moral lives. But with all good intentions they are committing grossly evil acts every day. *They are not wicked people; they have a blind spot in their moral field of vision.* They cannot see the obvious evil that we do to animals because they have been taught that the imprisonment, torture, and murder of animals is not evil. We are all taught this at every turn: at home, at play, in our schools and universities, by our governments, and, most shamefully of all, in our houses of worship. One of the greatest scandals of all the ages is that our churches and synagogues, which have led so many heroic struggles to relieve suffering and combat oppression, teach that God approves of cruelty committed against God's most vulnerable children. If you suggest that perhaps God would not care to be portrayed as a the Commandant of history's largest and longest-enduring death camp, our rabbis, pastors, and theologians will look at you perplexed, and as soon as it dawns on them that you are not joking, they will begin to quote scripture. "God gave us dominion over the animals. He told Noah to eat meat. He demanded animal sacrifice. Jesus ate fish. Saint Paul said vegetarians have 'weak faith.' " And on and on. I believe that to blame God for our own cruelty is blasphemy, and it is chilling to see how eagerly our religious leaders and teachers assign God the responsibility for Singer's eternal Treblinka.

I grew up in a devout Southern Baptist family. Food was an important part of our church fellowship. On Sunday afternoons we would gather in the church social hall, or under the ancient oak trees in the churchyard, to enjoy the feast that the ladies of the church had spread before us. Before the first plate was passed, we would bow our heads and fold our hands as the pastor offered thanks to God for the food we were about to eat. The obscenity of thanking God for the suffering and death that were on our plates never occurred to any of us. We had all been corrupted, as had our church, by absolute power.

There is an old joke about a preacher who was walking through the woods when a bear jumped out from behind a tree and grabbed him. The terrified preacher bowed his head and fervently prayed, "Lord, please hear my prayer and make this bear a Christian bear." When he looked up he was amazed to see the animal standing with folded paws and bowed head. "Lord," the bear said, "I thank Thee for this food which I am about to receive."

* * *

The Bible can certainly be used to defend the human use and abuse of animals, just as it has been used to defend slavery, segregation, and the oppression of women and homosexuals. But we have learned to look beyond specific passages that appear to

justify the abuse of our fellow human beings to find in the Bible
a stirring call for kindness, compassion, and mercy for everyone
regardless of race, religion, nationality, gender, or sexual orientation. It is long past time for us to recognize that the Bible issues
that same call in regard to every sentient being, regardless of
species. Animals are God's children no less than we.

Speaking of most organized religion, Isaac Bashevis Singer
said, ". . . they interpret their religious books as being in favor
of meat-eating. Sometimes they say He wants sacrifices and the
killing of animals. But I think God is wiser and more merciful
than that. And there are interpretations of religious scriptures
which support this . . ."[11]

Notes

1. Letter to Bishop Mandell Creighton, dated April 5, 1887.
2. See Brestrup.
3. See Peter Singer, pp. 24–94, and Ryder, 1983.
4. See Amory; Baker. Statistics are from "Body Count: The Death Toll in America's War on Wildlife," by Norm Phelps, The Fund for Animals, New York, 2000.
5. See Mason and Peter Singer; Davis; and Eisnitz.
6. "The Letter Writer," in Isaac Bashevis Singer, p. 271.
7. Foreword to Giehl.
8. See Patterson, 2002.
9. Address to the plenary session of AR 2001, July 1, 2001.
10. Quoted in Free, p. 32.
11. Preface to Rosen (1987 edition).

2: Kill All the Women and Children

Those who use the Bible to justify the eternal Treblinka usually do so by pointing to specific passages that they believe demonstrate divine approval. They tell us that Genesis 9:3 grants us permission to eat meat. Or that in Acts 10, God told Peter he could kill and eat every kind of animal. There is certainly no shortage of such passages in the Bible. In Appendix 1, for example, I have catalogued thirty places where the Bible says that God commanded or approved of animal sacrifice, and my list is not exhaustive.

For those who believe in the divine inspiration of the Bible, this might seem like an irrefutable argument. Thirty times the Bible says that God approved of using animals for religious sacrifice. That would appear to leave little room for discussion. As a fundamentalist bumper sticker puts it, "God said it, I believe it, and that settles it." What more is there to say?

As it happens, quite a bit. When we look into it more deeply, we see that things are not nearly as uncomplicated as that catchy slogan would have us believe. One complication that presents itself is numerous passages in the Bible that tell us that God approved, or even commanded, conduct toward other human beings that today no civilized person would countenance.

13

Ethnic Cleansing

Numbers 31 describes God ordering the children of Israel to undertake a retaliatory military raid against a rival tribe, the Midianites. In obedience to God's command, the Israelites "made war against Midian, just as the LORD had commanded Moses, and they killed every male." (Numbers 31:7) They took the women and children prisoner, which angered Moses, who told his officers to "kill every male among the little ones, and kill every woman who has known man intimately. But all the girls who have not known man intimately, spare for yourselves." (Numbers 31: 17–18) The Midianites were all to be exterminated, man, woman, and child, except for the young virgins, who were to be kept alive for the soldiers to rape, supposedly on God's orders.

In another graphic example, 1 Samuel quotes God as telling the Israelites, "Now go and strike Amalek and utterly destroy all that he has; and do not spare him; but put to death both man and woman, child and infant, ox and sheep, camel and donkey." (1 Samuel 15:3) Instead of following God's orders to the letter, the Israelites spared the Amalekite king, Agag, whom they took prisoner, and the most valuable of the animals, whom they kept for themselves as the spoils of war. This infuriated God, and the captured ruler was brought before Samuel, a prophet who served as God's spokesperson to the Israelites. "And Samuel hewed Agag to pieces before the LORD" to make amends. (1 Samuel 15:33)

Here we have two examples of "ethnic cleansing," or even genocide: punitive military raids—in the case of the Amalekites, conducted several generations after the original provocation—that include the mass murder of women and children, the hacking to pieces of a helpless prisoner, and the rape of young girls. And these are not unique incidents. There are at least ten other occasions on which we are told that the Israelites, presumably in obedience to God's command, exterminated in cold blood the entire civilian populations of towns or tribes whom they had defeated in battle.[1] Are we really to believe that the God of love and compassion described elsewhere in the Bible ordered these atrocities? Would any Jew or Christian today consider that these stories justify ethnic cleansing in the Balkans, genocide in Rwanda, or sectarian bombings in Northern Ireland? But using the fate of the Midianites, the Amalekites, and the rest to justify contemporary atrocities against human beings would be no different from using stories about God commanding animal sacrifice and approving of meat eating to justify the contemporary exploitation of animals.

When we read in the Bible stories of God commanding or condoning the killing of animals, we should remember these tales of barbarities that God is accused of ordering against human beings. If we do not regard these as justifying the mass murder of men, women, and children and the rape of young girls, why should we regard the former as justifying the imprisonment, torture, and killing of animals? Why should Biblical verses that show divine approval of animal abuse set an everlasting precedent while passages showing divine approval of the murder of men, women, and children do not? We cannot justify animal atrocities on the authority of the Bible unless we are also willing to justify human atrocities on the same basis.

Gentiles, Cretans, and Women

Turning to the New Testament, we have moved forward in time more than a thousand years, and the Bible writers' understanding of how God wants us to treat others has lost much of its savagery. There are no more tales of God ordering the mass murder of men, women, children, and animals, and the rape of virgins, just as there are none in the later books of the Hebrew Scriptures. But we still encounter attitudes that today are universally recognized as unworthy of men and women of good will.

In one such story, the gospels tell us that a gentile woman approached Jesus and asked him to cure her daughter of an illness. Jesus refused, saying, "It is not proper to take the children's bread and throw it to the dogs." When the woman responded that even dogs get to eat the crumbs that the children drop on the floor, Jesus relented and healed her daughter. (Mark 7:25–30) In a later chapter, we will consider what this story says about Jesus' attitude toward animals, but for the moment our concern is that this passage portrays him as a religious bigot who believed that gentiles were inferior to Jews. Would any Christian today argue that Jews are superior to non-Jews in any morally significant way? Or, reading it more generally, would any Christian today use this passage to defend any form of racism or religious discrimination? If not, what basis is there for relying on Biblical passages that seem to imply that animals are inferior to humans in ways that justify their abuse?

Another instance of racism in the New Testament occurs when Saint Paul says, "One of themselves, a prophet of their own, said, 'Cretans are always liars, evil beasts, lazy gluttons.' This testimony is true." (Titus 1:12–13) Are we to believe that God inspired Paul to the view that Cretans were all vicious liars and lazy gluttons, or was Paul merely reflecting a common prejudice of his day? And if Paul's view of a group of his fellow human beings could reflect cultural bias as opposed to divine inspiration, why not his view of animals as well?

In 1 Corinthians 11:3–9, Saint Paul argues that men may not cover their heads in church but women must do so because ". . . Christ is the head of every man, and the man is the head of a woman . . . he is the image and glory of God; but the woman is the glory of man . . . man was not created for the woman's sake, but woman for the man's sake." Later on, in chapter fourteen,

verses 34–35, he reinforces this view of women's innate inferiority. "The women are to keep silent in the churches; for they are
not permitted to speak . . . If they desire to learn anything, let
them ask their own husbands at home; for it is disgraceful for a
woman to speak in church."

Few Christian denominations still require women to wear a
hat or scarf when they enter the church sanctuary. Most recognize that in establishing this requirement, Paul was reflecting
not God's eternal truth, but a cultural bias against women that
was nearly universal in the ancient world. But an identical
cultural bias against animals was even more widespread in Paul's
society. If women can enter a sanctuary with their heads uncov-
ered in spite of this unequivocal Biblical injunction, why cannot
animals be spared the abuse that they suffer based on Biblical
injunction?

Likewise, if Paul's directive against allowing women to
"speak in church" were followed, most of our churches would be
in desperate straits for Sunday School teachers. Even the Roman
Catholic Church, which prohibits women from entering the
priesthood, allows them to address congregations that lack a
full-time priest. The Southern Baptist Convention, which
recently issued a nonbinding recommendation to its member
churches not to ordain women as pastors, nonetheless recognizes the vocation of those whom individual Southern Baptist
churches choose to ordain. Most other Christian denominations
accept women into their clergy in open disregard of Paul's directive, and even the theologically conservative world of televange-
lism features several popular female evangelists. If this unmistakable Biblical imperative can be ignored on the grounds that it
reflects a cultural bias rather than God's will, why cannot the
same principle be applied to passages, including passages written
by Paul, that just as plainly reflect a cultural bias against animals?

Slavery

The best example of a practice of which the Bible approves, but which Jews and Christians today consider morally repugnant, is human slavery.

In Leviticus 25:44–46, we are told that God specifically authorized slavery. "As for your male and female slaves whom you may have—you may acquire male and female slaves from the pagan nations that are around you . . . You may even bequeath them to your sons after you, to receive as a possession; you can use them as permanent slaves." Exodus, Leviticus, and other books of the Hebrew Scriptures establish rules for the treatment of slaves. Often these rules are intended to mitigate the suffering of slaves, but they carry no hint that human slavery is wrong on principle and ought to be abolished. In this respect, the Bible's position on slavery has much in common with the animal protection philosophy known as "animal welfarism," which holds that we may exploit animals for our own purposes, but that we should do so "humanely," and try to mitigate their suffering as much as is consistent with the purpose for which we are using them. Likewise, the Bible teaches a slave protection policy that we may call "slave welfarism": we may keep slaves in bondage and use them for our own purposes, but we should treat them as kindly as possible. No Jew or Christian today would regard slave welfarism as an adequate response to the moral challenge of human slavery, even though it is undeniably what the Bible teaches. Why, then, should we regard animal welfarism as an adequate response to the moral challenge of Isaac Singer's "eternal Treblinka?"

In regard to human slavery, the situation in the New Testament is no different from what we found in the Hebrew Scriptures. The institution of slavery is supported, but slaveholders are urged to treat their slaves humanely—slave welfarism. The New Testament book of Philemon is a letter from Saint Paul to a Christian slave owner, written on behalf of Philemon's runaway slave, a Christian named Onesimus. Paul, who was in prison at the time, sent Onesimus back to his owner, carrying the letter. Although his language does not make this entirely clear, it appears that Paul was asking Philemon to send Onesimus back to him as a personal slave for the duration of his imprisonment. The other possibility—which can also be argued but not proved from the text—is that Paul was asking Philemon to remit Onesimos' servitude. But if that is the case, Paul was doing so based on the friendship that he had formed with Onesimos, not as a matter of ethics or Christian teaching. Never once did Paul even hint that as a Christian Philemon ought not to own slaves. Quite the contrary: he expressly acknowledged Philemon's right to decide Onesimos' fate.

That Paul did support slavery is clear from another of his epistles, in which he says, "*Urge* bondslaves to be subject to their own masters in everything, to be well-pleasing, not argumentative." (Titus 2:9) In Ephesians, Paul expresses the same idea even more sharply, "Slaves, be obedient to those who are your masters according to the flesh, with fear and trembling, in the sincerity of your heart, as to Christ." (Ephesians 6:5) According to Paul, Christian slaves are to serve their owners as enthusiastically as they serve Christ! Four verses later, Paul asks slaveholders not to be cruel to their slaves, but never implies that Christian slave owners should free their slaves as a matter of Christian love, and never suggests that slavery might be an evil institution. One of my forebears was a Baptist minister in rural Tidewater Virginia. In 1837, he wrote a letter to the governor seeking permission to teach "Slaves and free Negroes" to read and write, giving the justification that if slaves could study scripture they would realize that God wanted them to obey their owners and not rebel or run away. If they took it at face value, indeed they would.

People anxious to rescue the New Testament from its own position on human slavery and the status of women sometimes claim that Paul's statement in Galatians 3:28 that "There is neither Jew nor Greek, there is neither slave nor free man, there is neither male nor female; for you are all one in Christ Jesus" means that slavery should be abolished and women granted equality with men. In point of fact, Paul intended nothing of the kind. As reading the entire passage makes clear, he was affirming that slaves and women, *like gentiles who choose not to be circumcised and become Jews*, may become Christians in spite of their inferior social status. Paul's point here has nothing to do with the institution of slavery or the role of women. He is simply arguing that gentiles ("Greeks" in his terminology) do not have to submit to circumcision in order to be accepted into the Christian community any more than slaves would have to be set free or women would have to become men. One's place in society, Paul is saying, is no impediment to full membership in the community of Christ. He makes the same point even more explicitly when he says, "Each man must remain in that condition in which he was called. Were you called while a slave? Do not worry about it; but if you are able also to become free, rather do that. For he who was called in the Lord while a slave, is the Lord's freedman; likewise, he who was called while free, is Christ's slave . . . Brethren, each one is to remain with God in that *condition*² in which he was called." (1 Corinthians 7:20–24) Becoming a Christian while a slave did not necessarily condemn you to lifelong slavery. If for some reason your owner offered to free you, there was no need to refuse. But otherwise, Jews should remain Jews, gentiles should remain gentiles, and slaves should remain slaves.

Today, it is often claimed that in the past the Bible was "misused" or "misinterpreted" to support slavery. But, as we have just seen, both the Hebrew Scriptures and the New Testament contain passages that explicitly approve of slavery, while *there is no passage in the Bible that condemns slavery or says that it ought to be abolished.* The defenders of slavery who quoted specific Biblical passages in support of their evil institution were "right" in precisely the same sense that modern defenders of animal exploitation who quote specific Biblical passages are "right." There are many places where the Bible does, indeed, say that these practices have divine approval, and no amount of creative translation or sophisticated interpretation can explain away that uncomfortable truth. Therefore, anyone who believes that animal exploitation is ethically acceptable because the Bible approves of it should, if they are to be consistent in their use of the Bible, also believe that human slavery is ethically acceptable—not to mention ethnic cleansing, genocide, and rape.

But in a deeper sense, those who used the Bible to defend slavery were indeed wrong, and among the first to point that out were religious abolitionists such as George Fox in England and William Lloyd Garrison, Lucretia Mott, and Maria W. Stewart in the United States. Inspired by the Bible's message of universal love and compassion, they led the crusade against human slavery until it was abolished in the nineteenth century. Episcopal Bishop John Shelby Spong rightly reminds us that "[The] 'Word of God' fueled every human movement for justice from the fight to end slavery and segregation to the feminist movement to the peace movement to the gay and lesbian rights movement. That Word of God challenges the prejudice that grows out of our limited knowledge, our tribal identities, our economic systems, and our sexual fears."[3] That same Word of God can also inspire us to challenge the prejudice born in the corrupt pleasure we take in our power over nonhuman animals. Our synagogues and churches can, and should, lead the crusade against animal slavery and slaughter just as they once led the crusade against human slavery and segregation.

* * *

Paul's wholehearted defense of slavery derives from his general theory of social and political power structures. "Every person is to be in subjection to the governing authorities," Paul tells us. "For there is no authority except from God, and those which exist are established by God. Therefore whoever resists authority has opposed the ordinance of God; and they who have opposed will receive condemnation upon themselves."[4] He goes on to explain that only criminals have anything to fear from governments, while those who do good have no cause for concern, a mystifying claim when you recall that Jesus, Stephen, and the other early Christian martyrs were put to death by these same governments. He goes on to tell us that every government ". . . is a minister of God, an avenger who brings wrath on the one who practices evil," and that Christians must "be in subjection" to them "not only because of wrath, but also for conscience' sake." (Romans 13:1–5)

Judged by this standard, the Magna Carta and the Declaration of Independence are profoundly anti-Christian documents. By this standard George Washington, Benjamin Franklin, Thomas Jefferson, and the other patriots who declared our independence from Great Britain were "opposing an ordinance of God," i.e., an "existing authority" in the form of the British crown, and if they had been caught and hanged, they would have brought this punishment on themselves. How many Christians today believe that Washington, Jefferson, Franklin, and the others deserved to be hanged as traitors? But that is precisely what Paul is saying. Even more chillingly, if there is "no authority except from God," the Third Reich and the Soviet Union were "ministers of God . . . avengers bringing wrath on the one who practices evil." Would any Christian today suggest that the Jews and Gypsies, liberals and democrats brought the gas chambers and gulags upon themselves? Or that Hitler and Stalin were "God's ministers and avengers?" But that is once again what Paul is saying. Were the imprisonment, torture, and death of people like Dietrich Bonhoeffer and Raoul Wallenberg "God's wrath on the one who practices evil?" Was the holocaust an act of God? As incredible as it seems, that is what Paul is telling us.

If Christians can universally condemn the Soviet and Nazi Treblinkas in spite of this Biblical teaching, why can they not equally condemn the eternal Treblinka of the animals?

Notes

1. These are described in Joshua 6:21, 8:18–29, 10:20–40, and 11:10–23. Joshua 11:20 tells us that God deliberately "hardened [the] hearts" of these tribes so that they would resist the Israelite attacks and give the Israelites an excuse to exterminate them.

2. The NASB italicizes words that do not appear in the original text but are necessary in English. This situation arises frequently because of differences in modes of expression between the ancient languages and English.

3. Spong, p. 75.

4. That is, they will have brought their punishment on themselves.

3: Cruelty is Atheism

All inspired scriptures, including the Bible, are produced by a divine/human collaboration. God has never penned a line or typed a page. That task has always been left for human hands.[1] And no project that depends on human agency has ever been perfect or ever will be. Therefore, the Bible, like all inspired scriptures, is an amalgam of divine inspiration and all-too-human intrusion. Divinely inspired though they were, the people who wrote the Bible were still vulnerable to the influences of their time, their place, and the events and debates they were caught up in. However perfect the message may have been at the point of transmission, at the point of reception it was subject to all manner of "static" and "line noise" in the form of the personal biases and cultural conditioning of those who received the inspiration and reduced it to writing. In the previous chapter we heard some of that static and line noise.

Dr. Roberta Kalechofsky, a Jewish scholar and animal protection advocate, speaks of the Hebrew Scriptures as "a stream of traditions," that includes much that does not reflect the ethical ideals of Judaism. But she does not for that reason hold it any less precious as a source of inspiration and guidance.[2] Reverend J. R. Hyland, an evangelical Christian minister, expresses a similar insight this way: "The coexistence of opposing viewpoints is a great strength of the Old Testament; it is one of the reasons for its continuing impact on the human race. The Hebrew Scriptures record both the continuity and the changes that took place in Judaism's understanding of God. They tell of the struggle between opposing values that continued for many centuries."[3] Speaking of both Testaments, Bishop John Shelby Spong, whom we quoted in the previous chapter, says that "the Bible is the Word of God in that it touches universal, timeless themes. The Bible is not literally true in a thousand details. But the Bible does touch the deep wells of truth, and to those deep wells it calls us again and again."[4]

The Bible was written over a period of more than a thousand years by hundreds of different authors living in dozens of different historical and cultural settings. Even many of the individual books that make up the Bible are the product of multiple authors and editors, most of whose identities are unknown and who often expressed sharply opposing views. The Bible is not a unified, consistent, internally coherent document, such as a modern book of theology or history might be; it is a dialogue in which we hear many different voices. The Bible is like a raucous neighborhood meeting discussing a contentious topic, with the participants all talking and shouting at once.

The Bible comprises a record of what sincere, but fallible, spiritual seekers—authors, editors, and compilers—believed to represent the inspiration of God. It is a description of revelation, but it is not the revelation itself, which occurs within the minds and souls of individual men and women. "The map," as the saying goes, "is not the territory." The Bible is a collection of maps often drawn by people who had traveled deep into the territory of revelation; but in undertaking that journey, they did not—they could not—completely abandon the land that the rest of us inhabit, and so their maps are composites of authentic inspiration, personal passions and prejudices, and social customs—amalgams of the spiritual, the individual, and the cultural. And just as the shouting of children can drown out the quieter conversation of adults, passion and custom often overwhelm inspiration, even in the most saintly. The Bible tells us that God speaks in a "still, small voice," (1 Kings 19:12, KJV) but the passions and prejudices of the world roar like a tornado and rumble like an earthquake. The wonder is not that the writers and editors of the Bible did not always capture the message in its pristine purity, but that they captured it at all.

Was Samson Antisocial?

According to a news report in 2001, Dr. Eric L. Altschuler of the University of California, San Diego has "diagnosed" the ancient Biblical hero Samson as "a classic case of antisocial personality disorder."[5] Samson lived during a time—around 1075 BCE—when the Israelites were second class citizens carrying on an intermittent, low-grade guerrilla war against their more powerful neighbors on the southern coastal plain of Palestine, the Philistines. Samson's mother dedicated him from birth to the service of God, as a token of which Samson was never to allow his hair to be cut. As long as his hair grew long, God would bless Samson with superhuman strength.

The young Samson married a Philistine woman. At the wedding banquet, he made a bet with some Philistine guests; if they could solve a riddle he posed for them, he would give them thirty suits of clothes. By threatening her family, the Philistines frightened Samson's new wife into telling them the answer. Enraged when he discovered the treachery, Samson murdered thirty Philistine men, stripped the corpses, and used their clothes to pay off the bet. His bride's father responded by annulling the marriage and arranging his daughter's wedding to a Philistine man. In one of the most egregious acts of animal cruelty and wanton destruction recorded in the Bible, Samson retaliated by catching three hundred foxes, tying flaming firebrands to their tails, and setting them loose in Philistine grain fields, vineyards, and orchards. Outraged, the Philistines kept the cycle of violence going by executing Samson's ex-wife and her father. We might expect Samson to be happy with this turn of events—after all, the Philistines were now killing each other—but he seems to have taken it as a personal insult, and he went on a rampage, murdering an unspecified number of Philistines and then hiding in a remote cave. Unable to find Samson, the Philistines prepared to massacre Jews indiscriminately, inspiring the leaders of the Jewish community to send an expeditionary force to capture Samson and surrender him to the Philistines. Samson went voluntarily, and when the Jewish soldiers turned him in, he used his extraordinary strength to break the ropes with which he was tied. Seeing the jawbone of a donkey lying on the ground nearby, Samson picked it up, used it to club one thousand Philistines to death, and made his getaway. In recognition of his great exploits, the Jews appointed him a "judge," a kind of tribal chieftain, a leader of the Israelite people, which he remained for twenty years.

Eventually, Samson developed a passion for another Philistine woman, Delilah. Bribed by the Philistine rulers, who were still nursing grudges from two decades earlier—and possibly from more recent offenses that we have no knowledge of— Delilah inveigled Samson into telling her the secret of his abnormal strength. Armed with this intelligence, Philistine soldiers slipped into Delilah's bedroom while Samson was sleeping there, cut off his hair, took him prisoner, and gouged out his eyes. But while he languished in a Philistine prison, Samson's hair grew back, the significance of which failed to register on his keepers. During a religious festival, the blind Samson was led into a temple for the sadistic amusement of the celebrants. On learning where he was, Samson asked his guard to place one of his hands on each of the two central pillars supporting the temple. Then, with a prayer to God, he gave one last terrible display of his strength by pulling down the columns and causing the crowded temple to collapse, killing himself and more than three thousand Philistines with him.[6]

Samson is a study in the futility of violence. Killing led to more killing, which led to still more killing. As I write this, more than three thousand years later, Jews and Arabs are killing each other in Gaza—the site of Samson's final act of slaughter—in the same pattern of attack and counterattack that blinded Samson and led him to a murderous suicide. But despite this, in both Judaism and Christianity, Samson is typically regarded as a man of great faith and a hero of the Jewish people, albeit a flawed hero.[7] Remarkably, Samson's tragic flaw is generally not seen as a vengeful and violent disposition, but as a lust for women that sometimes overcame his good sense. Dr. Altschuler's interpretation is a decided improvement over the traditional one, but he still does not have it quite right. Samson was antisocial only by the standards of today's society. He was typical of the society in which he lived, noteworthy only because of his great strength. He was, if you will, a projection of his world onto a larger screen. Samson was not at war with his own community, as happens when someone is antisocial; he was at war with the enemies of his community, which is a far different thing. If, as Doctor Altschuler says, "He wound up blind, dead, and friendless," that was only because he had the misfortune to fall into the hands of his community's enemies. Back among his own people, he was hailed as a hero and respected as a leader. After his death, Samson's relatives retrieved his body and buried it with honor among the graves of his family. Samson did not suffer from antisocial personality disorder. Ancient societies suffered from antisocial personality disorder.

This social pathology was not a trait only of the Jews and Philistines. It was the norm throughout the ancient world. Most of ancient history is a chronicle of atrocities piled upon atrocities, some committed by individuals, the majority by governments. The ancient world was a place where slavery, rape, torture, and murder were favored instruments of policy, both domestic and foreign. This was the nearly universal model of ancient society.

Viewed in this light, the story of Samson can help us understand more precisely the nature of the Biblical "stream of traditions" to which Dr. Kalechofsky referred and the "opposing viewpoints" alluded to by Rev. Hyland. The bulk of the Bible, both the Hebrew Scriptures and the New Testament, reflects the various societies—primitive Israelite, pre- and post-exilic Jewish, Greco-Roman—that produced it, societies that to a greater or lesser degree all replicated this "antisocial" model. This is natural and inevitable. But what is so remarkable, what has caused the Bible to endure as a source of inspiration down through the ages, is that it does not *just* reflect this selfish, cruel, and callous standard. Over the centuries, the Jewish people produced a remarkable number of great spiritual visionaries. Some of their names—as in the case of the Later Prophets, for example—we know. Others—such as the author of "You shall love your neighbor as yourself"—we do not. And these visionaries challenged the "antisocial" model of society in terms that still inspire us today.

A popular bumper sticker from the 1970s asked us to "Subvert the dominant paradigm." That is precisely what these inspired heralds of a higher truth did. They rejected the dominant paradigm of their society and injected into the Bible a call for a radically different way of understanding God, living our lives, and organizing society. As we shall see in the chapters that follow, they said that love, not self-interest, should rule individuals and nations. Where the dominant paradigm said that we should offer sacrifices to God (or the gods) because if we didn't he (or they) would visit us with plague and famine, they said that we should love God because God *is* love and love is the highest state to which we can aspire. Where the dominant paradigm said that we should do unto others before they do unto us, these holy messengers said that we should do unto others as we would have them do unto us. Where the dominant paradigm said that piety consisted of ritual, and righteousness lay in advancing the interests of ourselves, our family, and our tribe, they told us that piety consisted in loving God and loving the world that God had created, while righteousness lay in loving our fellow travelers through that world as much as we love ourselves.

And so in the Bible we find mixed in with the rumble and roar of the dominant paradigm, the still small voice of the most exalted message ever announced to humanity. It is that message, and that message alone, that makes the Bible the Western world's earliest, greatest breakthrough in humankind's unending search for God and goodness. God is always manifest; God is always available to us. When we cannot see God, it is not because God has hidden from us, but because we cannot see through the fog of our own appetites, desires, fears, and customs. I am absolutely certain that those who rejected the dominant paradigm of the ancient world to bring us the message of unbounded love and compassion had in fact connected with God and were conveying to us a divine revelation. There is no other way to explain a message that is so sublime and so contrary to our natural instincts.

Through a Glass, Darkly

To be sure, these bearers of divine inspiration did not always apply it to all beings—even to all human beings—or to all circumstances. As we have seen, the Bible regularly falls short of putting its fundamental principles into practice in concrete situations such as the treatment of captured populations and human slavery. But they got the underlying principles right. Their struggle to understand their own vision—and we today are still struggling to understand it, and all of its implications—illustrates the truth of Saint Paul's description of divine inspiration: "We know in part, and we prophesy in part . . . for now we see through a glass, darkly . . ." (1 Corinthians 13:9,12, KJV)

There is an old popular song that goes "You've come a long way from St. Louie, but baby, you've still got a long way to go." That is our situation with regard to human beings. Although we are still a long way from living up to the Bible's ideals, we have made great progress. Jews and Christians now universally condemn slavery and the harshest forms of oppression of women, generally condemn ethnic and racial intolerance, and are moving toward creating full equality for women and ending discrimination against homosexuals. Despite some truly atrocious historical events, the eighteenth through the twentieth centuries were actually a time of unparalleled progress in applying the Bible's message of love and compassion to all of humanity, thanks to the Enlightenment concept of rights. But with regard to animals, the journey has hardly begun. There are only a few lone voices crying in the wilderness. Learning to overcome appetite and custom so that we can love our nonhuman neighbors as ourselves is the great ethical challenge facing Judaism and Christianity in the twenty-first century. In fact, it is the great ethical challenge facing all of humankind, and Judaism and Christianity, because of two fundamental teachings that we shall examine in the next chapter, can play a vital role in showing us the way.

Notes

1. Exodus 31:18 tells us that God personally engraved instructions on two stone tablets (presumably the original Ten Commandments; see Deuteronomy 4:13) and gave them to Moses. But in a fit of anger, Moses threw them down on the ground and shattered them before anyone else saw them. (Exodus 32:19) The shattered tablets were replaced by new ones said to be dictated by God and engraved by Moses. (Exodus 34:27–28)

2. Presentation to the Farm Animal Reform Movement's Animal Rights 2000 Conference in Tysons Corner, Virginia, July 3, 2000.

3. Hyland, p. 5.

4. Spong, pp. 75–76.

5. Norton, Amy, "Doctors Diagnose the Bible's Samson as Antisocial," Reuters Health news service, carried on the Health News page of Yahoo!News, February 26, 2001.

6. The story of Samson is told in Judges 13–16.

7. Hebrews 11:32 includes Samson in a list of heroes who gained God's approval by their great faith. Disappointingly, all those mentioned by name were men of violence.

4: The Prime Directives

To hear God's still, small voice over the roaring and rumbling, we need a standard of interpretation that will help us distinguish genuine inspiration from static and line noise. We need a guiding principle that will help us distinguish God's message from human prejudices and passions. We need a way of testing the many diverse teachings and stories in the Bible against the most profound insights of the Jewish and Christian faiths.

Fortunately, this guiding principle is close at hand. Both Judaism and Christianity teach that a virtuous life stands upon two pillars: love for God and love for one another. Love for God is commanded most succinctly in Deuteronomy 6:5: "You shall love the Lord your God with all your heart and with all your soul and with all your might." Love for one another is directed in Leviticus 19:18: "You shall love your neighbor as yourself." In the Talmud and the subsequent rabbinic tradition, these two concepts, commonly known as *piety*, love for God, and *righteousness*, love for our neighbor, form the basis of all Jewish practice.[1] In Christianity, Jesus made these same principles the foundation of Christian virtue by calling them "the foremost" of the commandments and stating that "On these two commandments depend the whole Law and the Prophets." (Matthew 22:34–40; see Mark 12:28–34; Luke 10:25–28) *By citing "You shall love the Lord*

your God with all your heart and with all your soul and with all your
might" and "You shall love your neighbor as yourself" as the touchstones
of true religion, Jesus and the Talmud are telling us to understand the
Bible in the way that most clearly and fully reflects the love of God and
the love of our neighbor. If these are the foremost of the commandments, then all of the other commandments are subordinate to
them and must be consistent with them to be valid. Any statement—whether in the Bible or outside of it—that contradicts
these two commandments cannot represent divine inspiration.

Saint Paul reaffirmed this principle when he said, "For the
whole Law is fulfilled in one word, in the *statement* 'YOU SHALL
LOVE YOUR NEIGHBOR AS YOURSELF. ' "² (Galatians 5:14) And
again, when he said in Romans, "Owe nothing to anyone except
to love one another; for he who loves his neighbor has fulfilled
the law." (Romans 13:8)

If we apply this principle of interpretation to the Bible,
when we come across a passage that says God ordered the mass
murder of the Amalekites, including women and children, we
will ask, Is this consistent with the teaching that we should love
each other as much as we love ourselves? Or does this reflect the
passions and customs of warlike, tribal societies such as those
that flourished in the Middle East three thousand years ago?
The answer is obvious, and we understand immediately why this
story does not justify ethnic cleansing, genocide, or rape: it
violates what Judaism and Christianity alike regard as the Bible's
most fundamental, most universally valid, ethical teaching.
When numerous passages condone human slavery, we will ask, Is
this consistent with loving our neighbor as ourselves? Or does it
reflect an attitude of acquiescence to a practice that was so
ancient and universal that the writers of the Bible never thought
to question it? Once again, the answer is obvious, and we see
why the Bible's approval of slavery does not justify that barbaric

institution. Human slavery violates the Bible's most fundamental ethical teaching.

This is the same test that we must apply when we come across a passage that commands animal sacrifice or condones slaughtering animals for their flesh. Is this consistent with loving God with all our heart, with all our soul, and with all our might, and with loving our neighbor as ourselves?

To those who might object that I am trying to pick and choose what I will accept from the Bible and what I will reject, I plead guilty. Everyone who looks to the Bible for inspiration and guidance either picks and chooses a way around its contradictions and moral lapses or relies upon forced and improbable interpretations to resolve them; these are the only two choices the Biblical dialogue gives us. What I am suggesting here is that we pick and choose according to the two fundamental teachings of Judaism and Christianity. In regard to human beings, that is what most Jews and Christians already do, whether consciously or not, as witness the examples of women and slavery. I am simply proposing that we extend this tried and true principle, *which has been responsible for all of our ethical progress since the Bible was written*, to nonhuman animals.

You Shall Love the Lord Your God

Obviously, to love God with all our heart, with all our soul, and with all our might means to hold deep feelings of devotion and reverence. But it also means something more. Whenever we truly love, we have an overwhelming urge to translate the affection and devotion that we feel into concrete actions that benefit those we love. We want to nurture them, comfort them, care for them; we want to shield them from suffering and give them happiness. That urge is an essential part of love; if it were lacking, our love would more resemble selfishness. We would be taking pleasure and comfort, but giving nothing in return. We would be applying the name "love" to what was in reality only enjoyment; we would simply have found another way to love ourselves, and we would be using those we "love" as a means of benefiting ourselves. Love that does not express itself concretely for the benefit of those we love is self-love masquerading as genuine love.

God exists on a plane to which we cannot extend our love in any of these concrete ways, and moreover, being perfect, God has no need of our nurture, comfort, care, or gifts. God is the deity who has everything, and so there is nothing that we can give God. We can love God concretely only by loving God's creation. And if we love God's creation, we will nurture it, comfort it, care for it. *The "dominion" or "stewardship," that the Bible tells us God has given us over the other living beings in the world is simply an opportunity to love God concretely by protecting and nurturing God's creation.*

Obviously, protection and nurture mean different things for different kinds of creatures. In most cases, it is entirely appropriate to protect and nurture insentient creatures as a class. Except in special circumstances, we protect forests, not individual trees; we protect grasslands, not single blades of grass; and lakes and rivers, not drops of water. But with sentient creatures, it is different. Because they have been created with the ability to know pleasure and pain, to find joy in life and to fear death, they need protection and nurture as individuals. The life of the deer who is about to be killed by a hunter is as precious to him as my life is to me. The fact that the deer population is not "threatened" by the death of that deer is no more relevant than the fact that the human population would not be "threatened" if someone were to murder me. And because it was God who gave him the love of life, I love God concretely when I decline to hunt the deer. When I kill him for pleasure, I show disrespect for his creator.

In the Jewish tradition, the notion of loving God by loving God's creation is enshrined in the rabbinical doctrines of *bal taschit*, "not destroying" (traditionally interpreted as referring to the environment), and *tikkun olam*, "healing the world," according to which we have an obligation to express our love for God by preserving and healing the world that God has given us.[3]

The Christian tradition has typically been less open than the Jewish tradition to the idea of loving God by loving creation, owing to the greater influence of Greek philosophy, which we shall discuss in connection with Saint Paul. Still, it is very much present. In his *Homilies*, Saint Basil the Great (330–379), Bishop of Caesaria and a vegetarian, said, "We remember with shame that in the past we have exercised the high dominion of humankind with ruthless cruelty so that the voice of the earth, which should have gone up to Thee in song, has been a groan of agony. May we realize that they [animals] live not for us alone, but for themselves and for Thee and that they love the sweetness of life."[4] Alice Walker, best-selling author of *The Color Purple*, placed this same idea within the modern framework of social justice: "The animals of the world exist for their own reasons. They were not made for humans any more than black people were made for whites or women were made for men."[5]

In the Catechism of the Catholic Church, issued by Pope John Paul II as an authoritative statement of Catholic doctrine, the section on our ethical obligations toward the environment and animals is entitled "Respect for the Integrity of Creation," which is the same concept—expressed in more formal language—that is contained in the Jewish teachings on *bal taschit* and *tikkun olam*. If we love God, we will preserve and heal God's creation.

The Catechism's treatment of animals provides a good illustration of how most branches of Judaism and Christianity accept the fundamental concept of our ethical obligation to animals, but fall woefully short in the application by adopting a philosophy of animal welfarism. On the one hand, the Catechism says, "*Animals* are God's creatures. He surrounds them with his providential care. By their mere existence, they bless him and give him glory. Thus men owe them kindness." (2416) But the next paragraph takes away what the first has given. ". . . It is legitimate to use animals for food and clothing. They may be domesticated to help man in his work and leisure. Medical and scientific experimentation on animals is a morally acceptable practice if it remains within reasonable limits and contributes to caring for or saving human lives." (2417) In the first passage, the underlying principle of loving God by preserving and healing God's creation is affirmed, but in the second, the Catechism refuses to apply this principle whenever human interests are at stake. Respect for the integrity of creation ends where human benefit or pleasure begins. Our own selfish interests are allowed to override our love for God.[6]

We need to look at the fundamental ethical teachings of the Bible with eyes that can see where they have been taught not to look. Like the ancient prophets, we must subvert the dominant paradigm. We must have the honesty and courage to follow the Biblical principles to their natural conclusions, and not draw up short whenever those conclusions threaten our enjoyments, our creature comforts, or our cherished habits. A wrong act is not made right because the perpetrator benefits from it. Most unethical acts are committed to benefit the perpetrator. If this were the test, might would make right and in fact, as we have already noted, that is precisely the situation we are in regarding animals. That is the nature of the corruption of power that Lord Acton spoke of: If we have enough power, we eventually come to believe that whatever we do is right. That is why except in cases of immediate and severe necessity—direct defense of self or others—*the test of the morality of an act is never its benefit to the perpe-*

trator, but always its effect upon the victim. In regard to acts committed against humans, this is obvious to anyone. If I robbed you, no one would claim that this was an ethical act because I enjoyed spending your money. And so, if I steal an animal's life, why should that become ethical because I enjoy eating her flesh? Cruelty is cruelty, whether or not it results in human benefit.

When we eat meat, wear fur or leather, hunt or fish, experiment on animals, visit a zoo, or attend a circus with animal acts, we contribute to the suffering of God's sentient creation for our own pleasure or benefit, and in so doing, we fail to love God in the only concrete way that we can. We fail to preserve and heal God's sentient creation. We pridefully put ourselves first and relegate God to second place.

Seen from this perspective, animal rights is a way of living with humility according to God's plan, an idea expressed by the saintly Father Zossima in *The Brothers Karamazov*, the masterpiece of Russian Orthodox novelist Fyodor Dostoyevsky: "Love the animals: God has given them the rudiments of thought and joy untroubled. Do not trouble it, don't harass them, don't deprive them of their happiness, don't work against God's intent."[7]

You Shall Love Your Neighbor as Yourself

As to the second of the two fundamental Biblical teachings on how we ought to live, "You shall love your neighbor as yourself," we all have a natural tendency to do everything in our power to avoid suffering and find happiness for ourselves. This is what it means to "love yourself." It is an urge bred into the being of every living creature. To "love your neighbor as yourself" means to place her interests on a par with yours and to do everything within your power to alleviate her suffering and promote her happiness as energetically and persistently as you would your own. *This is the most radical idea ever introduced into the human dialogue.* As a guiding principle for ethical behavior by individuals, organizations, governments, and whole societies, it has never been improved upon in the more than three thousand years since it was first made, and I am confident that it never will be improved upon.

* * *

In the *Star Trek* television series and movies, Star Fleet commanders who visit other worlds are bound by a standing order not to interfere in the natural development of alien civilizations. This order, known as "the Prime Directive," overrides every other Star Fleet command. It must always be obeyed regardless of operational exigencies, even if that means the failure of the mission. Always, the Prime Directive reigns supreme. It is the ultimate guide to conduct. There are no exceptions.

"You shall love the Lord your God with all your heart and with all your soul and with all your might" and "You shall love your neighbor as yourself" are the Prime Directives of the Bible. According to Jewish and Christian tradition, they reign supreme. They are the ultimate guide to conduct. There are no exceptions.

Who Is Our Neighbor?

The most important advance in ethical thought since Leviticus was written has been to expand our definition of "neighbor." Once upon a time, "neighbor" meant "family"; then it came to mean "tribe"; now it tends to mean "race," "nationality," or "religion." In more "enlightened" circles, it has come to mean "humanity." In the twenty-first century, it is time to recognize that our neighborhood includes all sentient beings.

In Genesis 2:7 and 2:19, the Bible tells us that at creation God gave human beings and animals the same "living soul." As adjuncts to this living soul, God gave animals sense organs, a nervous system, and a brain able to process physical and emotional feelings—pleasure and pain—in ways similar to ours. By doing this, God made animals our neighbors. *It is not sharing a common humanity that makes us neighbors, any more than it is sharing a common race, religion, or ethnicity; it is possessing the same living soul and sharing a similar ability to experience suffering and joy.*

St. Thomas Aquinas, the thirteenth-century monk whose theological system, known as Thomism, is the closest thing the Catholic Church has to an official philosophy, denied not only that animals are our neighbors, but that we have any direct obligation to show them kindness. His argument, derived from Aristotle, was that we have direct moral obligations only to beings who are "rational," which is to say, beings who are capable of abstract reasoning. Since in Aquinas' view only human beings are rational, we have no direct moral duties to animals.[8] In 1789, the Enlightenment philosopher Jeremy Bentham elegantly refuted St. Thomas' argument against considering animals our neighbors with these words, "What else is it that should trace the insuperable line [between beings who are entitled to moral consideration and those who are not]? Is it the faculty of reason, or perhaps the faculty of discourse? But a full-grown horse or dog is beyond comparison a more rational, as well as a more conversable animal, than an infant of a day, or a week, or even a month old. But suppose the case were otherwise, what would it avail? The question is not Can they *reason*? nor Can they *talk*? but Can they *suffer*?"[9]

John Wesley, the founder of Methodism, also rejected Aquinas' claim. "What then is the barrier between men and brutes? The line which they cannot pass? It was not reason. Set aside that ambiguous term: Exchange it for the plain word, understanding: and who can deny that brutes have this? We may as well deny that they have sight or hearing."[10]

Cruelty is cruel to whomever it causes suffering, and kindness is kind to whomever it brings comfort, regardless of their species. For that simple reason, none of the traits that are alleged to distinguish us from animals could rightly exclude them from being counted as our neighbors. As Bentham noted, if animals lacked language, they would still be capable of suffering and joy. If they lacked the capacity for abstract reasoning, animals would still be capable of pleasure and pain; they would still love life and fear death. It is the sentience of the living soul that dictates how we ought to treat our fellow creatures. *All who share with us the divine spark of conscious life, given by God at creation, are our neighbors. All fall under the protection of the commandment to love them as we love ourselves.* Dr. Humphrey Primatt, an Anglican clergyman, put it this way in a book entitled *A Dissertation on the Duty of Mercy and the Sin of Cruelty to Brute Animals,* published in 1776: "Pain is Pain, whether it be inflicted on man or beast. And the creature who suffers it, being sensible to the misery of it, whilst it lasts, suffers evil." And we who inflict it, inflict evil.

Following the teachings of Hillel the Great, Judaism recognizes "You shall love your neighbor as yourself" as the foundation of Jewish ethics. Hillel himself explained its practical application and established its preeminence when he was asked to describe Judaism in the time a person could stand on one foot. "Do not do to someone else what you would not want done to you," he replied. "The rest is commentary. Go and study."[11] The rabbinic tradition applies this notion to animals in the doctrine of *tsar ba'ale chayim,* "the suffering of the living," which makes it a religious duty for Jews to do whatever they can to alleviate the suffering of animals.

Jesus applied this verse to daily life in terms similar to Hillel's. "In everything, therefore, treat people the same way you want them to treat you, for this is the Law and the Prophets." (Matthew 7:12; see Luke 6:31) Humphrey Primatt recognized that in this context "people" cannot be restricted to human beings, but must include every creature able to benefit or suffer from our treatment of them. He applied the Golden Rule to animals this way: "But let this be your invariable rule, everywhere, and at all times, to *do unto others as, in their condition, you would be done unto.*" (Emphasis in original.) If we were in the condition of the animals, that is to say, at the mercy of beings infinitely more powerful than we, we would not want those awesome creatures to imprison and kill us for our flesh and our skin, torture us in laboratories for the benefit of their own health or vanity, shoot us from ambush for sport, or lock us in tiny cages isolated from our fellows and bully us into doing tricks for their amusement. When we do these things to animals, we break the Golden Rule.

In summary, if we follow the Bible's teachings on love for God and love for our neighbor to their natural conclusion, we will respect the right of animals to live out their lives according to the natures with which God endowed them, free from interference by us.

These are the interpretations of the Bible to which Isaac Bashevis Singer alluded, interpretations that apply the Prime Directives of Judaism and Christianity—love of God and love of neighbor—as deeply and universally as we are able, so that no being to whom God has given the ability to feel pain and pleasure, to love life and fear death, is excluded. "We may pretend to what religion we please," said Reverend Primatt, "but cruelty is atheism."

Notes

1. While the distinction between "righteousness," meaning love of neighbor, and "piety," meaning love of God, is traditional, "righteousness" is also sometimes used to encompass both love of God and love of neighbor. To avoid confusion, I will always use "righteousness" in the narrower sense.
2. The translators of the NASB place quotations from the Hebrew Scriptures in small capitals.
3. Pronounced roughly BAHL tah-SHEET and tih-KOON oh-LAM. See Kalechofsky, 1998, pp. 6, 9, 27. Also, "Kindness to Animals" by Aviva Cantor et al. in Kalechofsky, 1992, p. 26 ff., and "Sounds of Silence" by Eric Katz in Kalechofsky, 1992, p. 56 ff.
4. Quoted in Wynne-Tyson, p. 9.
5. Foreword to Spiegel.
6. For an insightful discussion of the Catechism from a Christian animal rights standpoint, see Linzey, 2000, p. 56 ff.
7. Dostoyevsky, p. 383. (Book Six: "The Russian Monk" Chapter Three: "Conversations and Exhortations of Father Zossima"). I am grateful to Vasu Murti for reminding me of this passage.
8. Aquinas was opposed to animal cruelty, but on the grounds that it predisposed people to violence against other humans.
9. Bentham, p. 311. Emphasis in original.
10. Wesley, p. 3.
11. Babylonian Talmud, Tractate Shabbat, 31A. Cited in Hilton and Marshall, p. 17. Hillel taught during the reign of Herod the Great, 37–4 BCE.

5: The Image and Likeness of God

The closest the Bible comes to giving a definition of human nature is to say that we are created in the "image and likeness" of God (Genesis 1:26; see also 9:6), a claim that defenders of animal exploitation seize on to explain why we are entitled to use and abuse animals for our own purposes. I call this argument the "aristocracy theory" of creation, because it portrays human beings as the aristocrats of the universe whose privileged position in the divine scheme entitles us to reduce the rest of the earth's population to serfdom. When animal advocates point out that we are causing sentient beings terrible suffering and premature death, the "aristocrats" simply shrug their shoulders. "That may be true," they reply, "But it doesn't matter, because animals are not made in God's image." The question then becomes, How is that relevant? Why should only beings who are created in God's image be entitled to our love, compassion, and protection? And, more importantly, why should beings created in God's image be entitled to act in the most cruelly selfish ways toward everyone else on our planet? Is that what it means to be created in God's image, to have the right to create an eternal Treblinka for billions of defenseless sentient beings? If so, what does that say about God, whose image we are supposedly reflecting?

In fact, the aristocracy theory cannot be found in the Bible, which never suggests that being created in the image of God is a license to terrorize, torture, and kill. Nowhere does the Bible say that creation in God's image confers any sort of privileged moral status whatsoever upon humankind. The aristocracy theory is a later invention concocted to remove animals from the moral dialogue for the obvious reason that if they are included in it, animal exploitation will soon be seen as indefensible. Once you admit that animals are entitled to moral consideration, our treatment of them can only be seen as immoral. The aristocracy theory is a prime example of how we have been corrupted by our power over animals; its only purpose is to show that our might is right.

A Hierarchy of Service

So what does it mean to be created in the image of God? Clearly it. does not mean that we look like God, because no one any longer believes that God is a physical being with a physical appearance. Some theologians, most notably Saint Thomas Aquinas, have tried to demonstrate that reason is the characteristic that we and God share in common. We are created in God's image in the sense that we have a "rational soul," which reflects the defining attribute of God: rationality. But we have already discussed reason as a basis for considering another being deserving of our love and compassion and found it sorely wanting. As Bentham said, the question is not whether animals can reason but whether they suffer. Furthermore, the New Testament identifies quite clearly God's defining attribute, and it is not reason or rationality. 1 John 4:8 tells us that "The one who does not love does not know God, for God is love." And farther on, "God is love, and the one who abides in love abides in God, and God abides in him." (1 John 4:16) We do not reflect the image and likeness of God in our ability to reason, but in our ability to love.

Anglican theologian Andrew Linzey turns the "aristocracy theory" on its head. In Professor Linzey's view, we are not an aristocracy, but a priesthood. In fact, he tells us, humanity is "uniquely commissioned to exercise a self-sacrificial priesthood, after the one High Priest [i.e., Christ] not just for members of their own species, but for all sentient creatures." Linzey describes our priestly role in ringing terms: "The uniqueness of humanity consists in its ability to become the servant species."[1] Roberts Kalechofsky describes being made in the image of God as a call to "the highest moral behavior, not the lowest," and cites the mystical tradition of Kabbalah, which defines God in terms of divine activity, in support of this view.[2] To be created in the image of God is a summons to behave insofar as we are able with the godlike qualities of universal love and compassion.

Saint Paul expresses this idea in Christian language when he says, ". . . you [Christians] laid aside the old self with its *evil* practices, and have put on the new self who is being renewed to a true knowledge according to the image of the One who created him . . ." (Colossians 3:9–10) In the Garden of Eden, being created in the image of God may have been a fact, but after the fall from grace and the expulsion from the Garden, it is a fact no more; it is, Paul tells us, a process, and one that takes place through changes in our "practices." Through this process of continuing "renewal," we ever more clearly reflect the nature of God in our behavior. We reveal the image of God in ourselves when, and to the extent that, our lives are expressions of love. To Paul, as to the Jewish sages, being created in the image of God is a challenge to become better than we are, not an excuse to remain nastier than we need be.

* * *

It is hard to see how creation in the image of God can be thought
to justify depriving God's weaker children of their freedom, their
joy, and their lives. To claim that it does is to argue that God is
by nature cruel, selfish, and insensitive. As I said earlier, I
believe that claims such as this slander God and are unworthy of
anyone who is trying live in accordance with the Prime Directives. The Jewish tradition holds that "By definition, God is the
Compassionate One."[3] As we just noted, according to the Christian tradition, "God is love," which is simply another way of
saying the same thing. If this is so, then those who are created in
God's image are called to infuse our lives with love and compassion. We are called to protect, nurture, and comfort all of our
neighbors, all sentient beings who possess a "living soul," not
enslave, torment, and kill them. Contrary to the arrogant
pretensions of the aristocracy theory, the hierarchy established
by our creation in the image of God is a hierarchy of service, not
of privilege. Power does not entitle us to oppress the weak, it
obligates us to serve them. We owe the animals voluntary
service. Instead, we demand from them involuntary servitude.

* * *

In our arrogance, we have named ourselves *homo sapiens*,
"humanity the wise." If the scientific classification system had
been devised by pigs, geese, elephants, or any other species of
nonhuman animal, what would they have named us? Does
anyone believe that it would be "humanity the wise"? "Humanity
the loving"? "Humanity the compassionate"? Or "humanity the
godly"? More likely they would have dubbed us "humanity the
hateful," "humanity the vicious," or "humanity the cruel."
Perhaps, as Isaac Singer suggests, they would simply call us

"Nazis." Suppose for a moment that the angels adopted the aristocracy theory and treated us the way we treat animals. Would we believe that they were reflecting the image of a loving, compassionate God? Would we believe that they were angels or demons? Would they, in fact, be angels or demons? And which should sincere Christians and Jews want to be in the eyes of those over whom we have absolute power?

The Psalmist has given us the model that we should follow in trying to reflect the image of God onto a world tormented by violence, "O Lord, you preserve man and beast." (Psalm 36:6)

Dominion

Along with creation in the image of God, "dominion" is the Biblical concept most often invoked to explain why exploitation of animals is acceptable when exploitation of humans is not. According to Genesis 1:28, at creation God directed humankind to "Be fruitful and multiply, and fill the earth, and subdue it; and rule over the fish of the sea and over the birds of the sky and over every living thing that moves on the earth."

This verse expresses three distinct ideas. The first is that humanity should "be fruitful and multiply, and fill the earth," guidance that is frequently cited in opposition to birth control and population planning, blithely ignoring the fact that what may have been good advice when there were only two human beings on the planet is a prescription for disaster when there are six billion of us and the world population is exploding exponentially. In this century, we are crowding one another with an intensity that stresses our individual sanity and collective civility; we are driving other species out of their God-given homes while consuming resources and degrading the environment at a rate that threatens to make our planet unlivable. To say that under present circumstances God wants us to continue behaving in this manner is to say that God wants us to destroy ourselves, the earth, and all of the earth's other citizens along with us. We have to recognize that some of the instructions given in the Bible were meant for the moment, not the ages.

The second element in Genesis 1:28 directs humankind to "subdue" the earth, a notion that is widely called into action to defend unrestricted urban and industrial development and the wanton extraction of natural treasures. The Hebrew word used here is *kabash*, which appears more than a dozen times in the Hebrew Scriptures, usually with the meaning of subjugating or enslaving, once with the meaning of overcoming (sinful impulses), and once with the meaning of raping a woman.[4] Unlike the commandment to be fruitful and multiply, this was not even good advice at the time it was given. In the most ancient times, the region in which this command originated was so rich with vegetation and animal life that it became known as the Fertile Crescent. Vast forests and grasslands teemed with lions, leopards, bears, and other wildlife. But by the time of Jesus, most of the Middle East had been deforested, the wildlife had vanished, the topsoil had eroded, and much of the region had been reduced to the barren desert that we know today. The effort to "subdue" nature destroyed nature. Unfortunately, this sequence was not unique to the ancient Middle East. In fact, it represents a depressingly common pattern.

Civilizations arise by exploiting the natural wealth around them; as their prosperity increases, so do their populations, stressing their environment beyond its capacity to sustain them. Over time, the land is deforested, the wildlife disappear, the soil erodes, and the civilization collapses.[5] In the past, this has been a tragedy for the humans and animals who lived in the denuded area, but there were always other places with lush forests and fertile grasslands where animals could flourish and new civilizations take root. Today, however, with our vaunted "global economy," we are on the verge of deforesting and eroding the entire planet. When that happens, there will be no place for the animals to go or new civilizations to spring up. The commandment to "subdue the earth" has always been a prescription for local suicide. Thanks to technology, it is now a prescription for planetary suicide.

That is the practical effect of it. From an ethical standpoint, this injunction to subdue the earth, with its strong implications of raw force, cannot be reconciled with either of the Prime Directives. We do not enslave those we love, and we do not love God by practicing massive violence against creation.

The third concept contained in Genesis 1:28 is that we are to "rule over" all living creatures on earth, which is often taken to mean that we have divine permission to use animals for our own purposes with no need to concern ourselves with the quality of their lives or the nature of their deaths. The Hebrew verb *radah*, which the NASB translates "rule over," is translated in the King James Version as "have dominion over," which is why this concept is often referred to as *dominion*. In fact, *radah* simply means to "rule," "govern," or "have authority." It is used some twenty times in the Hebrew Scriptures to indicate the authority of governments over their citizens, a fact which is critical to understanding its meaning.[6]

We expect government officials to use their authority for the benefit of the people, not to satisfy their own lust for wealth or power. We use the term "public service" to indicate that the authority wielded by high officials is a kind of trust that they are obligated to exercise for the good of the citizens. And we harshly judge government officials who abuse their authority by oppressing their citizens to enhance their own status. In saying that we have dominion over nonhuman animals, the author of Genesis is telling us that they are analogous to citizens under our governance. If it is to be just, our dominion over animals must be exercised for their well-being, not for our own enrichment, convenience, or pleasure, just as the just dominion of governments is exercised for the well-being of the citizens.

Likewise, parents have authority over their children, but we expect them to exercise their parental dominion for the children's welfare. Parents who neglect the welfare of their children for their own convenience or benefit—as well as those who physically or psychologically abuse their children—we call unfit. *In the Judeo-Christian tradition, dominion that results in the oppression of the weak for the benefit of the powerful is always considered unjust. There is no reason why humanity's dominion over nonhuman animals should be judged by any other standard.*

The example given most frequently in the Bible of how human dominion over animals is supposed to work is a good shepherd tending his flock. To appreciate the significance of this, we have to recognize that the Bible always uses the image of a shepherd to represent nurture, protection, and selfless love. Even though the sheep may be ultimately destined for slaughter, this aspect of a shepherd's role does not enter into the Bible's use of the good shepherd as a metaphor. Therefore, when we consider what "good shepherd" means in Biblical imagery, we must put the notions of shearing and slaughter out of our minds; they were not in the mind of the author, and we would be reading into his image something starkly opposed to what he intended. The best known example of this in the Hebrew Scriptures is the Twenty-third Psalm, in which David speaks of himself as a sheep whose shepherd is God. "The Lord is my shepherd, I shall not want. He makes me lie down in green pastures; he leads me beside quiet waters; he restores my soul . . . I fear no evil for You are with me; Your rod and Your staff, they comfort me . . . Surely goodness and lovingkindness will follow me all the days of my life . . ." *The Twenty-third Psalm is the Biblical model for our dominion over animals.* Consistent with the Psalmist's theme, the Talmud teaches that "dominion" means "guardianship" or "stewardship," refers only to the use of animals for labor, and carries with it an obligation to kindness, compassion, and generosity.[7] In John 10:11, drawing on the imagery of the Twenty-third Psalm, Jesus tells us, "I am the good shepherd. The good shepherd lays down his life for the sheep." In Jesus' view, those who have dominion should place the well-being of those under their authority above their own interests to the point of being willing to die for them. The good shepherd will die for his sheep; he will not kill his sheep for his own benefit. Some may object that Jesus was using the good shepherd as a metaphor for himself, and did not mean it to be taken literally as a description of our dominion over animals. But the image of the good shepherd is not a valid metaphor unless it is also literally true. If Jesus had not believed that a good shepherd should hold the lives of his sheep more precious than his own life, he could not have used that image to describe himself.

* * *

One of the Bible's most telling comments about how God expects us to exercise our dominion over animals is found in Proverbs 12:10. "A righteous man has regard for the life of his animal. But *even* the compassion of the wicked is cruel." *By linking concern for animals with righteousness, this verse explicitly establishes that we have direct moral duties to animals.* Since the ancient author, traditionally held to be King Solomon, uses "righteous" in its wider meaning as someone who loves both God and neighbor, this verse applies both of the Prime Directives to our treatment of animals.

The observation that "even the compassion of the wicked is cruel" is especially relevant to the modern world. Circus trainers claim to love their performing animals. And yet, they use vicious iron hooks to break the spirit of elephants; they force terrified tigers to jump through flaming hoops; and they imprison wild animals in tiny cages with no room to move around for long hours every day. "Even the compassion of the wicked is cruel."

Dairy farmers claim to love their cows. They give them names, and the gentle animals come when called, filled with love and trust for the human who provides them with food and shelter. But this same human takes away their babies as soon as they are born in order to steal the milk, causing the cows to grieve like human mothers. The male calves are fastened into crates so small they cannot turn around and are fed an iron-deficient diet to keep their muscles from developing and getting "tough" or "stringy." While still babies, they are slaughtered for veal. As for their mothers, when they are too old and tired to get pregnant and give milk, they are sent to slaughter by the same farmer who used to look them in the eye and call them by name. "Even the compassion of the wicked is cruel."

Many people have dogs or cats who live like members of their families for years. The animals love them and trust them, and they will tell you that they love the animals. But one day, they buy expensive new furniture, and they can't afford to let the cat tear it up. Or they move to another city, and taking the dog just wouldn't work out. Or they have a baby, and she's allergic. Whatever the excuse, the result is the same. An animal who loves his companions and believes that he has a family for life is taken to the local shelter and abandoned. He is terrified and lonely, his heart is broken, and the odds are overwhelming that he will be killed, because very few people want to adopt an older animal. "Even the compassion of the wicked is cruel."

As we said earlier, these people commit wicked acts by ignorance, not intent. They have been taught not to see the suffering of animals, and it is this moral blind spot that sustains the eternal Treblinka.

* * *

The Catechism of the Catholic Church, whose view of animals we considered earlier, recognizes that dominion is subject to moral restraints when it says, "Use of the mineral, vegetable, and animal resources of the universe cannot be divorced from respect for moral imperatives. Man's dominion over inanimate and other living beings granted by the Creator is not absolute." (2415) Consistent with its animal-welfare orientation, the Catechism treats animals as "resources" and fails to distinguish categorically between moral imperatives applicable to sentient creatures and those applicable to insentient creation. But even so, the recognition that our dominion is in some way defined by moral obligations is an important step in the right direction. It is the thin edge of a wedge that may in time open the Catholic Church to the recognition that when God gave animals a sensitive "living soul," God also gave them the right to have that soul and that sensitivity respected. Minerals are "resources"; plants are "resources"; animals are living souls and sentient beings, just as we are.

In any event, the grant of dominion in Genesis 1:28 cannot be used to justify meat eating, because in the next verse, as part of the same instruction, we read, "Then God said, 'Behold, I have given you every plant yielding seed that is on the surface of all the earth, and every tree which has fruit yielding seed; it shall be food for you." (Genesis 1:29) *According to the Bible, at the time of giving humanity dominion over the animals, God also instructed us to maintain not just a vegetarian but a vegan diet, one that includes no animal products whatsoever*, a command that Genesis tells us stayed in effect until after the flood.

From a Biblical perspective, it was God who invested animals as well as humans with the ability to suffer and with the love of life. Surely, a just and merciful God would not want us to use our power to bring suffering to those whom God had entrusted to our care. Dominion is a delegated responsibility, a grant of trust from the creator to humankind to care for the whole of creation, including each individual endowed with the ability to suffer.

Notes

1. Linzey, 1995, pp. 45, 57.
2. Kalechofsky, 1992, p. 47.
3. Rabbi Shlomo Riskin, "Compassion or Concession," in Kalechofsky, 1992, p. 45.
4. Wigram, *Hebrew Concordance*, p. 586 (Strong number 3533). Brown, et al., p. 461.
5. See Ponting for a description and analysis of this process.
6. Wigram, *Hebrew Concordance*, p. 1158 (Strong number 7287). Brown, et al., p. 921. For a linguistic discussion of both "dominion" and "image and likeness," see Yoel L. Arbeitman, "In All Adam's Domain," in Kalechofsky, 1992, pp. 33–42.
7. Tractate Shabbat 119, Tractate Sanhedrin 7, cited in "Questions and Answers" by Richard Schwartz, in Kalechofsky, 1992, 224.

6: All God's Children Go to Heaven

A nother answer that defenders of animal slavery often give when we ask why it should be moral to exploit, abuse, and kill animals, but immoral to treat humans the same way, is that we have souls and they don't.

One response that jumps immediately to mind is, Why should that matter? In humans and animals alike, it is the mortal creature who dies, not the immortal soul. Therefore, it is wrong to kill any being who loves life and fears death, whether that being has an immortal soul or not. Furthermore, if animals do not have immortal souls, and this life is all they have to look forward to, that is all the more reason why we should not turn their only fleeting chance for joy into hell on earth.[1]

But having said this, we have to recognize that—contrary to a widespread prejudice—*the Bible teaches that animals do, in fact, have souls and will be present in the kingdom of heaven.*

Living Souls

In the story of creation, we are told that "God created the great sea monsters and every *nephesh chayah* [pronounced roughly nefesh hi-yah] that moves, with which the waters swarmed after their kind . . ." (Genesis 1:21) Then "God said, 'Let the earth bring forth [every] *nephesh chayah* after their kind, cattle and creeping things and beasts of the earth after their kind.' "

(Genesis 1:24) *Chayah* means "living," "alive." *Nephesh* means the animating force, the whatever-it-is that makes a person or an animal a conscious, sentient individual. My *nephesh* is what makes me uniquely me, and your *nephesh* is what makes you uniquely you. And our *nephesh* is what gives us both awareness and will. When our *nephesh* leaves our body, we die.[2]

A little farther on, Genesis tells us that "Then the LORD God formed man of dust from the ground and breathed into his nostrils the breath of life. And man became a *nephesh chayah*." (Genesis 2:7) And later still we are told that God brought all of the birds and land animals before Adam "and whatever the man called a *nephesh chayah*, that was its name." (Genesis 2:19) According to Genesis, *the life force, the divine breath that brings will and consciousness, is the same in animals as it is in human beings*. Tragically, our English Bibles hide this fundamental truth by translating *nephesh* one way when it refers to animals and another when it refers to humans.

The King James Version translates *nephesh chayah* in Genesis 1:21 and 24 as "living creature." Then in 2:7, where it refers to a human being, the KJV translates *nephesh chayah* as "living soul." But in 2:19, where it again refers to animals, *nephesh chayah* reverts to "living creature," obscuring the fact that the Bible makes no distinction between the nature of the living spirit with which God endowed humanity and that with which God endowed the animals. Unfortunately, most modern translators have followed suit, although in an apparent effort to head off precisely the argument that I am making here, they usually avoid the word "soul" altogether. The NASB, NIV, and the New Revised Standard Version, which are all Protestant sponsored, translate *nephesh chayah* as "living being" when it describes humankind and "living creature" when it describes animals, as does *Tanakh: The Holy Scriptures*, which is the translation of the Jewish Publication Society. The Catholic *New American Bible* is more circumspect, while still concealing the identical nature of the life force in humans and animals. It constructs the English sentence in verse 19 in such a way that *nephesh chayah* is translated "them."

Ancient translators, both Jewish and Christian, engaged in no such double talk. In Alexandria, Egypt in about 250 BCE, a team of rabbis and scholars translated the Hebrew scriptures into Greek for Jews living outside of Israel who could no longer read Hebrew comfortably. Known as the Septuagint, their work remained the standard Bible for Greek-speaking Jews for hundreds of years. When the New Testament quotes the Hebrew Scriptures, it most often quotes the Septuagint. In Genesis 2:7 and 2:19, in the reference to animals as well as the reference to humankind, the Septuagint translates *nephesh chayah* as *psyche zosa*. *Zosa*, like *chayah*, which it translates, means "living," "alive." *Psyche* is the word which the authors of the New Testament used to mean "soul."

Around 400 CE, Saint Jerome translated the Bible into Latin for use by Christians in the western Roman Empire who could not speak Greek. The Vulgate, as Jerome's Latin Bible is known, was used by the Roman Catholic church throughout the world until the Second Vatican Council and is still considered an authoritative Latin text. Although he consulted the Septuagint, Jerome translated the Hebrew scriptures directly into Latin from Hebrew, a language in which he was fluent. Both when it refers to animals and when it refers to humanity, St. Jerome translated *nephesh chayah*, as *anima viventis*. Like *chayah* and *zosa*, *viventis* means "living." *Anima* is the word that Jerome employed in the New Testament to mean "soul." Perhaps not coincidentally, Saint Jerome was a vegetarian.

Down to the present, *psyche* is the word used in the Greek Orthodox Church and other Greek-speaking churches to mean "soul," while *anima* is used for "soul" in the Latin literature and liturgy of Roman Catholicism. If you look up *nephesh* in a Hebrew-English dictionary of modern Hebrew, you will find the equivalent is "soul"; and if you look up "soul" in the English to Hebrew section, you will find the Hebrew equivalent is *nephesh.*[3]

Biblical dictionaries and other Christian reference works, however, often go to great lengths to hide or deny the Biblical teaching that animals have souls. To cite only two of many instances, *Strong's Exhaustive Concordance of the Bible*, originally published over a hundred years ago and still one of the most widely used Bible study aids in print, gives as its primary definition of *nephesh* ". . . a breathing creature." Not until eleven lines farther down is "soul" mentioned as an equivalent.[4] *Vine's Complete Expository Dictionary of Old and New Testament Words*, widely used by conservative Protestants, defines *nephesh* as "soul, self, life, person, heart" (i.e., when "heart" is used figuratively). But the author then goes on to claim that "soul," *although used to translate nephesh well over four hundred times in the KJV*, "is an unfortunate mistranslation of the term" because the ancient Jews allegedly had no concept that corresponded to our notions of a soul. Dr. Vine would rather have us believe that the concept of a "soul" was really "Greek and Latin in origin," than admit that Genesis tells us that animals have souls.[5] The popular *Zondervan Pictorial Bible Dictionary*, published by the Methodist Zondervan publishing house, is a bit more straightforward. After identifying *nephesh* as the Hebrew word for "soul," the author of the article goes on to say, "The difference between man and beast is not that man has a soul or spirit (Gen. 1:20, 7:15; Eccl. 3:21), but that man is created in the image of God, whereas the beast is not."[6] At least he acknowledges that animals have souls, even if he falls back on the "aristocracy theory" of creation in the image of God to draw an absolute distinction between human and nonhuman.

In the previous chapter, we quoted Proverbs 12:10: "A righteous man has regard for the life of his animal." The word that the NASB, along with most English Bibles, translates "life" is *nephesh*, and here we have another case of translators refusing to acknowledge that the Bible ascribes souls to animals, which this verse plainly does. It tells us that if we are righteous, we will recognize that animals are sensitive living souls, just as we are, and we will treat them accordingly. This verse would be more accurately translated, "A righteous man respects the soul of his animal." But since we modern folk are not inclined to use or likely to understand the phrase "respects the soul," a more accessible translation might be "A righteous man respects the personhood of his animal."

Covenants with the Animals

The description in Genesis of God infusing animals and humans with identical souls is reinforced by two passages in the Hebrew Scriptures that portray God as entering into covenants with the animals in the same manner as with humanity.

The first occurs immediately following the flood. "Then God spoke to Noah and to his sons with him, saying, 'Now behold, I Myself do establish My covenant with you, and with your descendants after you; and with every living creature [i.e., with every "living soul," every *nephesh chayah*] that is with you, the birds, the cattle, and every beast of the earth with you; of all that comes out of the ark, even every beast of the earth. I establish My covenant with you; and all flesh shall never again be cut off by the water of the flood, neither shall there again be a flood to destroy the earth.'

"God said, 'This is the sign of the covenant which I am making between Me and you and every living creature that is with you, for all successive generations . . . When the [rain]bow is in the cloud, then I will look upon it, to remember the everlasting covenant between God and every living creature [every *nephesh chayah*] of all flesh that is on the earth.' " (Genesis 9:8–16)

In making this covenant, the earliest recorded in the Bible, God does not distinguish among the "living souls" on earth. God's covenant is with all of us—human and nonhuman without distinction—all are recognized as being equally objects of God's concern and participants in God's covenant.

God's second covenant with animals is described in Hosea 2:18: "In that day [when Israel returns to righteousness] I will also make a covenant for them with the beasts of the field, the birds of the sky, and the creeping things of the ground. And I will abolish the bow, the sword, and war from the land, and will make them lie down in safety."

Humankind has failed to practice the dominion of love. Instead, we have exercised the dominion of selfishness, arrogance, and violence. Our power has brought fear and suffering to all the living souls on earth. And so, God makes a special promise to the animals—the innocent bystanders caught in the crossfire of humanity's moral failure—that some day humankind (represented in the prophet's words by Israel) will return to righteousness. Then the kingdom of heaven will be inaugurated, and the animals may "lie down in safety."

Like the covenant following the flood, this promised covenant testifies that animals have souls and are true objects of God's concern. But more than that, it is presented as a direct promise from God to the animals that they will take full part in the coming kingdom. Those who look forward to the kingdom of heaven need not worry about whether their beloved companion animals will be there to share it with them. *The animals have God's promise.*

The Peaceable Kingdom

The teaching that animals have immortal souls and will be present in the kingdom of heaven is given in more extended form in Isaiah, which describes the heavenly kingdom this way: "And the wolf will dwell with the lamb, and the leopard will lie down with the young goat, and the calf and the young lion will feed together; and a little boy will lead them. Also the cow and the bear will graze, their young will lie down together, and the lion will eat straw like the ox. The nursing child will play by the hole of the cobra, and the weaned child will put his hand on the viper's den. They will not hurt or destroy in all My holy mountain, for the earth will be full of the knowledge of the LORD as the waters cover the sea." (Isaiah 11:6–9)

Although some claim that the animals in this passage are merely symbolic and that no actual animals will be present in heaven, there is nothing in the text to support this view. It is an unsubstantiated claim put forward by people who wish to ascribe a uniqueness to humanity that is not taught in the Bible.

To the contrary, the logic of Isaiah's description requires that the animals be present literally. Isaiah is depicting the heavenly kingdom as a return to the Garden of Eden, where all living souls lived in peace and harmony with one another. How "the lion will eat straw like the ox" we do not know. Perhaps we will not enter heaven in our gross physical bodies, but in subtler, "spiritual" bodies, "glorified" bodies, as they are sometimes called. But however that may be, what we do know is that the participation of animals in the kingdom is meant literally. Every species of sentient living souls was present in the Garden, and they will all be present in heaven.

I have sometimes heard Christians object that animals will not be present in the kingdom of heaven because only those who have been redeemed by the blood of Christ can enter the heavenly kingdom. Since animals are not capable of accepting Christ as their savior, so this argument runs, they cannot be redeemed even if they do have souls, and so cannot be present in heaven. Saint Paul—normally not a friend of animals, as we shall see— specifically refutes this claim on three separate occasions by teaching that animals are, in fact, redeemed through Christ. In Romans 8:19–21, he says, "For the created universe waits with eager expectation for God's sons to be revealed . . . for the universe itself is to be freed from the shackles of mortality and enter upon the liberty and splendor of the children of God." (New English Bible)[7] All creatures, animals as well as human beings, are "God's sons," waiting for their divine nature to be revealed in the kingdom of heaven. They, like us, will enjoy the "liberty and splendor" of being "children of God." Indeed, according to Paul, the entire universe, and everything and everyone in it, will be transformed, which may explain how "the lion shall eat straw" in Isaiah's peaceable kingdom.

John Wesley took this passage as the scriptural text for his sermon "The General Deliverance," in which he taught that the animals will be present in heaven. "Away with vulgar prejudices, and let the plain word of God take place," declared the founder of Methodism. "They [animals] 'shall be delivered from the bondage of corruption, into glorious liberty' [Wesley is quoting from the KJV]—even a measure, according as they are capable—of the 'liberty of the children of God.' "[8] Wesley goes on to assert that a famous passage in the book of Revelation describing heaven applies as fully to animals as to humans. "God shall wipe away all tears from their eyes. And there shall be no more death, neither sorrow, nor crying. Neither shall there be any more pain: For the former things are passed away." (Revelation 21:4, KJV) "As a recompense for what they [animals] once suffered, while under the 'bondage of corruption,' " Wesley assures us, "When God has 'renewed the face of the earth,' and their corruptible body has put on incorruption, they shall enjoy happiness suited to their state, without alloy, without interruption, and without end."[9]

In Ephesians 1:9–10, Saint Paul again declares that Christ suffered and died for all of creation, including the animals. "And he [God] made known to us the mystery of his will according to his good pleasure, which he purposed in Christ, to be put into effect when the times will have reached their fulfillment—to bring all things in heaven and on earth together under one head, even Christ." (NIV, see note 46) Finally, in Colossians 1:20, Paul tells us straight out that God chose to "reconcile all things to Himself" through Christ.

For many, the Bible's teaching that animals have immortal souls and will be present in the kingdom of heaven is a great comfort. It tells us that we will be reunited with the beloved companions from whom we are now separated by death. It promises wonderful reunions and a sharing of love without which the bliss of heaven could never be complete. But there is another side to this promise as well. All of us who have eaten meat or drunk milk, all who have shot a deer or goose, all who have visited zoos and attended circuses with animal acts, have served as guards at Isaac Singer's eternal Treblinka. Our victims will be in heaven with us. What will we say when we are face to face, soul to soul, with those who needed our mercy and received only our arrogance? Will we say, "I'm sorry. I didn't know better"? Or perhaps, "I was never a big meat eater. Just on special occasions or when I had a craving." Or maybe, "I wanted to stop eating you, but whenever I said I was a vegetarian my family and friends all acted like I was some kind of a nut." Nothing we can say will be adequate.

Notes

1. The latter argument was apparently first put forward in 1776 by Reverend Humphrey Primatt, whom I have already quoted several times. See Linzey, 1991, p. 57.

2. Strong number 5315. See Brown et al., pp. 659–661. For a brief but excellent discussion of *nephesh* and animal souls, see Regenstein, pp. 43–44.

3. As, for example, in *The Contemporary Shilo Pocket Dictionary: Hebrew-English, English-Hebrew*, edited by Zevi Scharfstein, Shilo Publishing House, New York, 1963, English to Hebrew section, p. 217, where *nephesh* is the first equivalent listed for "soul," and Hebrew to English section, p. 149, where "soul" is the second listed equivalent for *nephesh*, behind "self."

4. Strong, "Hebrew and Aramaic Dictionary of the Old Testament," p. 95.

5. Vine, "Old Testament Section," pp. 237–8.

6. "Soul" by James Buswell, Jr., Ph.D. in Tenney, p. 807.

7. I have quoted the NEB here because Paul's Greek is convoluted and the NASB follows it so closely that the English is barely intelligible.

8. Wesley, p. 5.

9. Wesley, p. 6.

7: The Suffering of the Living

What does the Bible teach about our nonhuman neighbors? First, it tells us that they are sentient. By creating us as living souls, God made us all able to experience pleasure and pain, both physical and emotional. For ethical purposes, sentience is an absolute; one either has it—like humans and animals—or does not—like plants and rocks.[1] Whether one species has a higher level or more complex form of sentience than another species is irrelevant to the ethical question. It may be (or it may not be; we really don't know) that on some abstract, objective scale the more complex animals, mammals for instance, would turn out to be "more sentient" than, let us say, crustaceans. But even if that were true, it would be of no moral significance because *the lobster's pain and fear are as important to the lobster as my pain and fear are to me. Because of this, all suffering is of equal moral significance.* The lobster has the same right to live free of fear and pain as I do, because God has given him a desire to do so that is as strong as mine. And in this, he and I are bound together by something far more important than our myriad and striking differences. *The sentience that we share as living souls makes the lobster my neighbor.* And it generates for me the ethical obligation to love him as I love myself and to treat him as I would want to be treated if I were in his situation.

In Genesis 9:2 we read that animals can experience "fear and terror," which are signs of emotional as well as physical sentience, while in Joel 2:22, God comforts the cattle in a field by telling them not to be afraid, which would hardly be necessary if they could not experience fear. Psalm 104:29 describes animals as being "dismayed" (KJV, "troubled") when God does not provide for their needs, and Joel 1:18 depicts cattle and sheep as "suffering" because of a drought. As we shall see in the next section, Deuteronomy 25:4, "You shall not muzzle the ox while he is threshing" presumes that animals can suffer both physically and emotionally.

Secondly, the passages cited above presume that animals have a will, which is to say they have goals and want to attain them. Like us, they feel satisfaction when they attain their goals and frustration, or even despair, when they do not. It does not matter whether your highest goal is to write the great American novel or simply to find dinner and a safe place to sleep. *The lobster's goals are as important to the lobster as my goals are to me, and therefore, they deserve the same level of respect.*

Third, animals are intelligent. Proverbs 30:24–28 cites four examples of animals who, although physically small and weak, survive by being "exceedingly wise." These include ants, who have the forethought to lay aside food for the winter; rock oryx, whose front feet are not designed for digging burrows and have learned to live in clefts in the rock; and locusts, who organize large-scale, disciplined forays in search of food. In a similar vein, Jeremiah 8:7 speaks admiringly of the intelligence of various species of birds, who know when it is time to start their seasonal migrations. Rather than assuming, for no good reason, that these activities are the result of mindless "instinct" or, as we might say today, "genetic programming," the authors of these passages accept them for what they plainly are: products of intelligence. The intelligence of other species may differ from ours; it may be more narrowly specialized, perhaps; but it is uniquely suited to the physical capacities and needs of the creature possessing it.

Even so, for the sake of discussion, let us assume that some species may have a lower level of intelligence than others. *Having a lower level of intelligence does not make one less of a living soul.* A human being with an IQ of seventy is as much a living soul as Leonardo Da Vinci or Albert Einstein. When, as happens now and then, someone suggests otherwise, Jews and Christians are united in their outrage—as they should be. But if an individual's ability to create immortal art or decipher the mysteries of the universe is irrelevant to his or her standing as a living soul entitled to life, liberty, and the pursuit of happiness, why should a species' level of intelligence be morally relevant? *The Bible describes all of the animals of land, air and sea, including the birds, fish, reptiles, shellfish, and insects, as possessing identical living souls. It does not discriminate among them according to intelligence or a capacity for abstract reasoning.*

In the New Testament, Jesus attributes a fourth characteristic to animals: what we might call "the higher emotions," such as love, loyalty, and compassion. Contemplating the coming destruction of Jerusalem at the hands of the Romans, Jesus cried out, "O Jerusalem, Jerusalem, *the city* that kills the prophets and stones those sent to her! How often I wanted to gather your children together, just as a hen *gathers* her brood under her wings, and you would not *have it!*" (Luke 13:34) Looking for an image that conveyed the ultimate in selfless, nurturing love, Jesus chose not a human examplar, but a chicken.

* * *

The Bible's most important reference to the sentience and will of nonhuman animals is found in Deuteronomy 25:4, which became the scriptural foundation of the rabbinical doctrine of *tsar ba'ale chayim*, "the suffering of the living," which makes relieving the suffering of animals a religious duty for Jews.[2] "You shall not muzzle the ox while he is threshing." The point of muzzling the ox was to keep him from eating any of the grain that he was threshing. The point of the commandment was the cruelty of forcing an animal to work for hours at a time with his face only inches from delicious food while not allowing him to eat any of it. From time immemorial, Jews have taken great pride in the care they provide their animals. We may assume that when this commandment was given, working animals were typically well fed during their "off hours." And so the writer is less concerned that the ox may be suffering serious hunger than that he will experience the emotional pain of being tantalized by the sight and smell of food that he cannot have. *This is a commandment to exercise the dominion of love by caring for the happiness as well as the health of animals.* It is a reminder to all of us who have companion animals that it is not enough to look after our friends' physical needs. We must also give them our companionship and provide enjoyable activities to occupy their minds.

God's concern for the suffering of animals is also enshrined in the Ten Commandments, where we read, ". . . the seventh day is a sabbath of the LORD your God; *in it*, you shall not do any work, you or your son or your daughter or your male servant or your female servant or your ox or your donkey or any of your cattle or your sojourner who stays with you . . ." (Deuteronomy 5:14. See Exodus 20:10.) This commandment is also given in Exodus 23:12, where the reason for including the animals is explicitly stated. "Six days you are to do your work, but on the seventh day you shall cease *from labor* so that your ox and your donkey may rest, and the son of your female slave, as well as your stranger, may refresh themselves."

The commandment to allow working animals to rest on the sabbath presumes that they will be used for labor, which was the universal practice in the ancient Middle East. In this regard, it reflects a philosophy similar to the Catholic Catechism. It points us in the right direction by requiring us to ameliorate the suffering that we inflict upon animals for our own benefit, but it does not call on us to stop inflicting that suffering. It reflects an animal welfarist philosophy that fails to follow to its logical and necessary conclusion the path that it has started us on. Slave welfarism was morally superior to the belief that slave owners had no ethical responsibilities to their slaves; it led to an easing of their suffering, and forced people to think of slaves as fellow human beings. But in the final analysis, slave welfarism was morally incomplete—and therefore inadequate—because it permitted the cause of the suffering, slavery, to continue.

When slave welfarism ceased to be a way station on the road to abolition and became an end in itself, it degenerated into an ally of human slavery. Animal welfarism is no different. As a way station on the road to animal liberation, animal welfarism can ease the suffering of animals until the cause of that suffering, animal exploitation, can be ended. No less importantly, it forces people to think of animals as sentient beings who are able to suffer, and thereby brings liberation closer. But when easing the "unnecessary" suffering of animals who are being exploited for human benefit is taken to be the goal, then animal welfarism becomes an ally of animal abuse and an apology for the eternal Treblinka.

Until the industrial revolution, animal labor was universally practiced throughout the world. Noting that Jesus told his audiences to be alert to the "signs of the times," Reverend J. R. Hyland has suggested that the invention of machinery that has made animal labor obsolete throughout the industrialized world

can be seen as a sign that God wants us to end all of our exploitation of animals.[3]

* * *

The Hebrew Scriptures give us a striking indication of God's
concern for the well-being of animals in Exodus 23:4–5. "If you
meet your enemy's ox or his donkey wandering away, you shall
surely return it to him. If you see the donkey of one who hates
you lying *helpless* under its load, you shall refrain from leaving it
to him, you shall surely release *it* with him." In a rare lapse, the
NASB has garbled the English, but the idea is clear even if the
prepositions and pronouns are not. The obligation to help an
animal in distress must override even our strongest and most
deeply held passions and our most cherished notions of self-
interest. The ox and the donkey may belong to our enemy. It
may give us great pleasure and be to our benefit to allow our
enemy to lose the service of his animal. But the animal's claim on
our compassion takes precedence.

In the New Testament, Jesus enunciated a similar principle
when he endorsed the Jewish doctrine that it was proper to
break the sabbath to help a person or an animal in distress.
"Which one of you will have a son or an ox fall into a well," he
asked a group of scholars, "and will not immediately pull him out
on a Sabbath day?" (Luke 14:5) On another occasion, Jesus
remarked with approval that everyone who owned an ox or a
donkey worked on the sabbath by taking the animal out of his
stall and leading him to water. (Luke 13:15) In both cases his
point was the same: Our obligation to alleviate suffering, of
animals as well as humans, takes priority over our other religious
duties.

Later, we will see Saint Paul deny that God cares about
animals or that we have ethical duties toward them. But in

saying this, Paul contradicted both the Hebrew Scriptures and Jesus.

Notes

1. The Bible never refers to plants or minerals as "living souls."

2. Pronounced roughly tsar bah ah-lay hi-yeem; English spellings vary. For a thorough discussion, see Schwartz, pp. 15–39.

3. Hyland, pp. 65–68.

8: Your Hands Are Covered with Blood

A nimal sacrifice was the ancient equivalent of vivisection. Both are attempts to improve the lives of human beings by torturing and killing animals—in the first case by propitiating God and in the second by gaining knowledge. The fact that most people today believe that biomedical research is effective and sacrifice is not is irrelevant to the moral issue. Biomedical experiments on human beings would provide life-saving knowledge far more quickly and reliably than experiments on nonhuman animals, but we consider it immoral to sacrifice the freedom, health, or lives of individual human beings for the sake of finding cures to even such mass scourges as cancer and AIDS. The Nuremburg Convention, an international treaty inspired by the experiments Nazi doctors performed on Jews and other victims of fascism, prohibits medical experiments on unwilling or uninformed human subjects, no matter how great the benefit might be for the rest of the human race. Yet we do not hesitate to take the freedom, health, and lives of millions of nonhuman animals every year for reasons as trivial as trying to understand their sexual habits or to test the irritancy of a new shade of lipstick. If it is immoral to imprison, torture, and kill humans for the welfare of the human race, why is it not also immoral to imprison, torture, and kill animals for the same purpose?

One answer that Jews and Christians often give is that "God directed the Jewish people to kill animals to preserve their own well-being; therefore, it must be OK for us to do so as well. Only now, because we have a different understanding of how the physical universe functions, we conduct research instead of sacrifices."

An Odor Soothing to the Lord

There are many places where the Hebrew Scriptures portray God as approving, or even requiring, animal sacrifice. As early as the first generation born on earth, we are told that God preferred Abel's sacrifice of animals to Cain's offering of grain and vegetables, leading Cain to kill Abel in a fit of envy. (Genesis 4:3–5) Genesis 8:20–21 tells us that God approved of Noah's sacrifice of animals after the flood, while the New Testament describes Mary and Joseph as going to the Temple following the birth of Jesus to sacrifice two pigeons. (Luke 2:22–24) But the foundation of Jewish sacrificial worship is found in Exodus, Leviticus, and Numbers, and to a lesser extent Deuteronomy, which record the instructions that God is said to have given the Israelites during the forty years that they wandered in the wilderness of Sinai and Jordan after fleeing Egypt in the Exodus. For example:

> You shall also take the one ram . . . and you shall slaughter the ram and shall take its blood and sprinkle it around on the altar. Then you shall cut the ram into its pieces . . . You shall offer up in smoke the whole ram on the altar; it is a burnt offering to the LORD: it is a soothing aroma, an offering by fire to the LORD. (Exodus 29:15–18)

> He shall slay the young bull before the LORD; and Aaron's sons the priests shall offer up the blood and sprinkle the blood around on the altar . . . And the priest

shall offer up in smoke all of it on the altar for a burnt offering, an offering by fire of a soothing aroma to the LORD. (Leviticus 1:5–9)

But if his offering to the LORD is a burnt offering of birds, then he shall bring his offering from the turtledoves or from young pigeons. The priest shall bring it to the altar, and wring off its head and offer it up in smoke on the altar; and its blood is to be drained out on the side of the altar . . . And the priest shall offer it up in smoke . . . it is a burnt offering, an offering by fire of a soothing aroma to the LORD. (Leviticus 1:14–17)

Aaron [Moses' brother and the first high priest] and his sons laid their hands on the head of the ram. Moses slaughtered *it* and took some of its blood and put it on the lobe of Aaron's right ear, and on the thumb of his right hand and on the big toe of his right foot . . . Moses then sprinkled *the rest of* the blood around on the altar . . . Then Moses . . . offered them [the ram's flesh and other offerings] up in smoke on the altar with the burnt offering. They were an ordination offering for a soothing aroma; it was an offering by fire to the LORD. (Leviticus 8:22–28)

These passages, and others that I could quote, would have us believe that God enjoys smelling the smoke from the burning flesh of a dead animal as it rises to heaven. They would have us believe that God refused to nurture and guide the people unless they killed God's innocent creatures, dabbed themselves with blood, and splattered more blood over the sacred altar. They describe superstitious practices that the Israelites borrowed from the pagan religions of the tribes they encountered on their seemingly endless journey across Sinai and Jordan. They are part of the line noise that these terrified refugees, fleeing from Egyptian slavery headlong into the unknown, struggling every day against the brutality and uncertainty of life as a homeless people in the ancient wilderness, mistook for the voice of God. Killing in the name of God—whether the victim is an animal or a human—is always done out of fear and ignorance, never out of faith and wisdom; it violates the Prime Directives.

I Will Not Smell Your Sacrifices

Even in ancient times, there were those who recognized this. Beginning around 780 BCE and continuing for roughly three hundred years, the Later Prophets served as the conscience of the Jewish kingdoms. In many ways, they were the counterparts of modern muckraking journalists. In vehement, even virulent terms, they exposed the venality and corruption of the royal courts and the Temple establishment that supported them—the state religion, what we might call "official" Judaism—and issued a clarion call for a return to the simplicity and purity of the authentic and original Judaism. Rejecting the formalism of Temple worship, they taught that true piety is in the heart and mind, not in the performance of rituals. They attacked the greed and callousness of the ruling class, including the Temple priests, and they demanded justice for the poor and oppressed. Reeling off long litanies of the vices and cruelties of the kings and their cronies, they urged the powerful to repent and mend their ways, predicting dire consequences if they did not. The Later Prophets are among the most eloquent crusaders for social justice in all of history.

There is a slogan that animal rights activists often chant at demonstrations: "One struggle, one fight! Human freedom, animal rights!" It reflects two ideas that we discussed in chapter one: first, that all oppression is interconnected because all life is interconnected; and second, that all oppression, no matter who the victim may be, arises from the same mindset, and those who oppress one group will just as easily oppress another. Those who will abuse animals will also abuse humans, and vice versa. The Later Prophets understood this, and with the same fervor that they attacked the other sins of the ruling classes, they attacked animal sacrifice.

> "What are your multiplied sacrifices to Me?" says the LORD. "I have had enough of burnt offerings of rams and the fat of fed cattle; and I take no pleasure in the blood of bulls, lambs or goats. When you come to appear before Me, who requires of you this trampling of My courts? Bring your worthless offerings no longer, incense is an abomination to Me. New moon and sabbath, the calling of assemblies—I cannot endure iniquity and the solemn assembly. I hate your new moon *festivals* and your appointed feasts, they have become a burden to Me; I am weary of bearing *them*. So when you spread out your hands *in prayer*, I will hide My eyes from you; yes, even though you multiply prayers, I will not listen. Your hands are covered with blood. Wash yourselves, make yourselves clean; remove the evil of your deeds from My sight. Cease to do evil, learn to do good; seek justice, reprove the ruthless, defend the orphan, plead for the widow." (Isaiah 1:11–17)

The first thing we notice is that the prophet is refuting the passages in the Books of Moses, such as those we quoted above, that claim that God commanded animal sacrifice. Speaking on behalf of God, he asks, "When you come to appear before Me, who requires of you this trampling of My courts?"—clearly implying that no one does, and certainly not God. But secondly, and in some ways more importantly, the prophet directly links justice to animals with justice to human beings. "Cease to do evil, learn to do good," he has God tell the people. "Stop killing animals on the altar and start standing up for widows and orphans." Until they do, God will not hear their prayers, because their hands are covered with the blood of innocent animals. Further on, Isaiah returns to this theme, again linking the exploitation of animals and the exploitation of humans.

But he who kills an ox is *like* one who slays a man; he who sacrifices a lamb is *like* the one who breaks a dog's neck; he who offers a grain offering *is like one who offers* swine's blood; he who burns incense is *like* the one who blesses an idol. As they have chosen their *own* ways, and their soul delights in their abominations, so I will choose their punishments and will bring on them what they dread. (Isaiah 66:3–4)

Here the prophet equates animal sacrifice with human sacrifice. It is as much a sin, the prophet says, to sacrifice an animal as to sacrifice a human being. The fact that the grain offering is included in this condemnation does not detract from the prophet's attack on animal sacrifice. Isaiah is telling us that God does not want sacrifices of any kind. God wants mercy and justice—toward humans and animals alike.

Thus says the LORD of hosts, the God of Israel, "Add your burnt offerings to your sacrifices and eat flesh. For I did not speak to your fathers, or command them in the day that I brought them out of the land of Egypt, concerning burnt offerings and sacrifices. But this is what I commanded them, saying, 'Obey My voice, and I will be your God, and you will be My people; and you will walk in all the way which I command you, that it may be well with you.' " (Jeremiah 7:21–23)

This is a flat-out statement, not even phrased as a rhetorical question, that the "commandments" relating to animal sacrifice in Exodus, Leviticus, Numbers, and Deuteronomy are not the word of God. Jeremiah's words are unequivocal and leave no room for any other interpretation. But the NIV, the best selling English Bible in the world today, renders verse 22 differently. "For when I brought your forefathers out of Egypt, I did not just give them commands about burnt offerings and sacrifices, but I gave them this command: Obey me and I will be your God and you will be my people."

The Hebrew says, "I did not speak to your fathers," and then repeats for emphasis, "I did not command them." The Jewish translators of the Greek Septuagint and Saint Jerome in his Latin Vulgate understood this passage the way the New American Standard Bible renders it, as a flat denial that God had commanded sacrifices after the flight from Egypt. The KJV, RSV, NRSV, NEB, NAB, and THS agree. As far as I am aware, the New International Version stands alone.

Like Isaiah, Hosea condemns animal sacrifice not once, but twice. "For I desire mercy, not sacrifice, and acknowledgment of God rather than burnt offerings." (Hosea 6:6, NIV)[1] Two chapters later, the prophet has God say: "Since Ephraim has multiplied altars for sin, they have become altars of sinning for him . . . As for My sacrificial gifts, they sacrifice the flesh and eat *it, but* the LORD has taken no delight in them. Now He will remember their iniquity, and punish *them* for their sins; they will return to Egypt." (Hosea 8:11–13)[2]

In the first passage, the prophet states plainly that God does not want sacrifices and burnt offerings, but a change of heart and a change of behavior. The second passage is equally clear.

"Since Ephraim has multiplied *altars for sin*, they have become altars of sinning for him." In ancient Jewish worship, altars served only one purpose. They were used to offer sacrifices. Even the so-called "altar of incense" or "golden altar," whose primary purpose was the burning of incense, had the blood of sacrifices sprinkled on it during worship.[3] Since sacrifices could only be offered at an altar, multiplying altars meant multiplying sacrifices.[4] The sin being condemned here is animal sacrifice:

> I hate, I reject your festivals, nor do I delight in your solemn assemblies. Even though you offer up to Me burnt offerings and your grain offerings, I will not accept *them*; And I will not *even* look at the peace offerings of your fatlings. Take away from Me the noise of your songs; I will not even listen to the sound of your harps. But let justice roll down like waters and righteousness like an ever-flowing stream. Did you present Me with sacrifices and grain offerings in the wilderness for forty years, O house of Israel? (Amos 5:21–25)

The Hebrew verb translated "delight," *ruach*, literally means "breathe," "sniff," or "smell," and "smell" is how it is translated in the KJV.[5] Amos is directly refuting the claim often repeated in Leviticus that God enjoys the smell of dead burning flesh. In the last sentence—like Isaiah and Jeremiah—he emphatically denies that the Israelites had offered sacrifices during their forty-year pilgrimage across Sinai and Jordan following the flight from Egypt, again flatly contradicting the numerous passages in Exodus, Leviticus, Numbers, and Deuteronomy that claim just the opposite. Amos' message is the same as Hosea's. We please God by changing our hearts and our behavior; we offend God when we offer sacrifices.

With what shall I come to the LORD *and* bow myself
before the God on high? Shall I come to Him with burnt
offerings, with yearling calves? Does the LORD take
delight in thousands of rams, in ten thousand rivers of
oil? Shall I present my firstborn *for* my rebellious acts,
the fruit of my body for the sin of my soul? He has told
you, O man, what is good; and what does the LORD
require of you but to do justice, to love kindness, and to
walk humbly with your God? (Micah 6:6–8)

Again we find the same rhetorical questions, with the same
implied answer. God does not want sacrifices. God wants us to
follow the Prime Directives. We please God by loving God and
by loving God's children, all of God's children.

A Psalm of Compassion
Psalms is a book of hymns, many of which are traditionally
attributed to King David. Occasionally, the Psalms refer to
animal sacrifice in ways that reflect approval (e.g., Psalm 20:3).
But in one instance, the Psalmist—said to be David—condemns
sacrificial religion in terms reminiscent of the prophets. "Sacrifice and meal offering You have not desired; my ears You have
opened; burnt offering and sin offering You have not required."
(Psalm 40:6) [6]

A Clear Choice
The Bible forces us to choose. First, the Hebrew Scriptures tell
us that God commanded animal sacrifice and took pleasure in it.
Then the prophets and the Fortieth Psalm tell us that God never
gave any such command and finds sacrifices abhorrent. Both
versions cannot be correct. We are witnessing an argument
between two incompatible schools of thought, and we have to
decide which to accept. The Prime Directives make that choice

an easy one. Killing our neighbor in the hope of improving our own lives cannot be reconciled with loving our neighbor as ourselves. It is a simple matter. And yet, the words of the prophets make the modern religious establishments as uncomfortable as they made the ancient religious establishments to whom they were originally directed more than 2,500 years ago.

Empty Sacrifices

Believers in the literal inerrancy of Scripture have concocted a theory to reconcile the prophets' condemnation of sacrifice with the Bible's repeated claim that God commanded it. Known as the "empty sacrifice" theory, it contends that the prophets are not condemning animal sacrifice *per se*, but only sacrifices that have degenerated into meaningless external rituals, unaccompanied by a true change of heart.

The first problem with the empty sacrifice theory is that it is contradicted by the plain meaning of the prophets' words. Each of these passages flatly condemns all animal sacrifice, not just sacrifice that is not accompanied by repentance. In straightforward language, they call for repentance *instead of* sacrifices, not repentance *in addition to* sacrifices. In fact, some call for repentance *for having offered sacrifices*: "Your hands are covered with blood."

The second problem with the empty sacrifice theory is that the passages from Isaiah, Jeremiah, and Amos make it clear that these prophets did not believe that sacrifice had ever been commanded by God. To those readers who may be disturbed by my observation in chapter two that along with authentic divine inspiration the Bible also contains "static" or "line noise," I would point out that these prophets, bearers of much of the Bible's inspired message, held the same view. They rejected in no uncertain terms the Bible's claims that God had commanded and approved of animal sacrifice. When their criticism of animal sacrifice is taken in concert with their frequent condemnation of "idol worship" and "chasing after false gods," it becomes clear that they considered animal sacrifice to be a sinful practice that had been absorbed from the idolatrous superstitions of Israel's neighbors; they considered it a betrayal of God.

From a Christian standpoint, the third problem with the empty sacrifice theory is that Jesus himself rejected it.

Matthew 9:13 quotes Jesus as saying to a group of Pharisees, "But go and learn what this means, 'I DESIRE COMPASSION, AND NOT SACRIFICE.' " A little farther on, Matthew has Jesus repeat this injunction to a Pharisee teacher in almost the same words. "But if you had known what this means, 'I DESIRE COMPASSION AND NOT A SACRIFICE,' you would not have condemned the innocent." (Matthew 12:7)

The Pharisees, a Jewish denomination that we know took part in animal sacrifice, must have explained the passages in which the prophets condemned sacrifices by some rationalization very much like the empty sacrifice theory. And so when some Pharisees accused Jesus of impiety because he sometimes shared meals with "sinners" and gathered food on the sabbath, both practices that they claimed were forbidden to pious Jews, he responded by pointing out their own impiety—sacrificing animals. "If you had known what this means," he told them, quoting Hosea 6:6, "you would not have condemned the innocent," referring to the innocent animals slaughtered for sacrifices. Jesus read Hosea's statement as a blanket condemnation of animal sacrifice and rejected alternative interpretations. Christian commentators today who espouse the empty sacrifice theory should listen more closely to the words of Jesus, "Go and learn what this means."

A Clean Bill of Health

Another occasion on which Jesus referred to animal sacrifice is described in Mark 1:40–45.[7] After curing a leper, Jesus told the man not to tell anyone about his miraculous cure, but to go to the Temple, offer the sacrifice prescribed for the curing of leprosy, and receive a priest's certification that he had been cured.[8] This is often cited as an instance of Jesus condoning animal sacrifice, but I do not believe that to be the case.

The ancients understood that leprosy was contagious, but they did not understand how the contagion took place, and so they played it safe. They made lepers outcasts who had to wear distinctive clothing and warn anyone who approached them to keep their distance. Lepers were not permitted to work, shop in the marketplaces, or take part in the life of their family or community. They could have close contact only with other lepers. In Israel, a leper who had been cured could not re-enter society until he had gone to the Temple, been inspected by a priest, and been certified healthy. Unless the appropriate sacrifices were offered, the priest would not issue a bill of health, and the person would not be able to resume a normal life; he would have to continue living as a pariah and a beggar.

A few days before curing the leper, Jesus had conducted his first miraculous healing. A man suffering from mental illness had come into the synagogue at Capernaum in Galilee while Jesus was there and disrupted the services. Jesus cured the man. That evening people flocked to the house where Jesus was staying hoping to be cured of all kinds of physical and mental ailments. Many of them he cured, and his reputation as a healer spread like wildfire.

The leper whom Jesus cured on this occasion was not one of his followers who could be expected to share his beliefs, but simply someone who approached Jesus out of desperation because of his newfound fame as a healer. This celebrity seems to have worried Jesus because it drew attention away from his teaching mission. People were so impatient to be healed of their physical infirmities that they paid little attention to his spiritual message. And once they had been cured, they were so overjoyed that they seldom hung around to listen to his teaching. And so Jesus cautioned the man not to spread the word that he had cured him. Jesus knew that having once been cured, the man would not be willing to continue living as an outcast, as though he still had the dread disease. But without the certification of the priest, that is exactly what he would have had to do. And without the sacrifice—and without knowing how the man had been cured—the priest would not certify. And so Jesus told him, in effect, "I know you're going to the Temple to get your health certificate, so go on and do that, but at least don't tell anyone else that I cured you." Jesus was not directing the leper to offer the sacrifices; he knew that the man was going to do that no matter what he said. Jesus was instructing him not to tell anyone besides the priest how he had been cured.

* * *

There is only one other instance in which the gospels tell us that Jesus commented on animal sacrifice. When he identified the Prime Directives as the foremost of the commandments, a Pharisee scholar responded

> "Right, Teacher; You have truly stated that HE IS ONE, AND THERE IS NO ONE ELSE BESIDES HIM; AND TO LOVE HIM WITH ALL THE HEART AND WITH ALL THE UNDER-STANDING AND WITH ALL THE STRENGTH, AND TO LOVE ONE'S NEIGHBOR AS HIMSELF, is much more than all burnt offerings and sacrifices." When Jesus saw that he

had answered intelligently, He said to him, "You are not far from the kingdom of God." (Mark 12:32–34)

Not far. Only one short step remained. To recognize that sacrifices are not merely inferior to loving God and loving your neighbor, but that God does not desire them at all. The Pharisee espoused the empty sacrifice theory, and Jesus rejected it.

Jesus' opposition to animal sacrifice is stated more bluntly in the Ebionite Gospel, which was used by the early Jewish Christians and is now lost except for brief quotations in the *Panarion* of Epiphanius. Here, Jesus says, "I am come to do away with sacrifices, and if you cease not from sacrificing, the wrath of God will not cease from you."[9]

The First Animal Liberation

The gospels record numerous occasions on which Jesus visited the Temple to teach and debate, but they say nothing to suggest that he ever offered a sacrifice. What they do say is that he once drove from the Temple the money-changers and animal dealers who made their living from animal sacrifice. Matthew describes the incident, known as the "Cleansing of the Temple," this way. "And Jesus entered the temple and drove out all those who were buying and selling in the temple, and overturned the tables of the money-changers and the seats of those who were selling doves. And He said to them, 'It is written, MY HOUSE SHALL BE CALLED A HOUSE OF PRAYER; BUT YOU ARE MAKING IT A ROBBERS' DEN.' " (Matthew 21:12–13; see also Mark 11:15–17, Luke 19:45–46, and John 2:14–16) John tells us that sheep and oxen were also in the temple compound and Jesus drove them out as well.

The money-changers were there because only Jewish coins, which carried no "graven images" such as were forbidden by the Ten Commandments, could be used to pay for sacrifices. Since Greek and Roman money, which did carry graven images, circulated widely in Israel, the money-changers were needed to exchange Jewish coins for pagan. The animals were there to be sold to worshippers for use as sacrifices. Jesus' reference to the temple being turned from a "house of prayer" into a "robbers' den" is a quotation from Jeremiah 7:11, which is part of the same passage that contains the prophet's condemnation of animal sacrifice that we quoted above (Jeremiah 7:22). By liberating the intended sacrificial victims while quoting from a passage in the Hebrew Scriptures that condemns animal sacrifices, Jesus was making a frontal assault on the sacrificial system as well as on the practice of buying and selling in the Temple compound.

The cleansing of the Temple is history's first recorded civil disobedience conducted at least in part on behalf of animals, and Jesus was the first animal liberator. When Christian animal rights activists practice civil disobedience to release imprisoned animals, they are walking in the footsteps of Jesus and practicing the imitation of Christ.

The Last Supper

It is often claimed that Jesus must have taken part in at least one form of animal sacrifice because lamb is the prescribed main course at the Passover seder, and Matthew, Mark, and Luke describe the Last Supper as a seder. But nowhere in the New Testament is it stated, or even implied, that lamb was served at the Last Supper. In fact, the gospel accounts strongly suggest that the main course of the meal was bread.[10] The claim that Jesus ate lamb at the Last Supper is based entirely on the assumption that he must have followed the traditional practice for a seder. But the gospels portray Jesus as frequently provoking the anger of the religious authorities in Jerusalem by refusing to follow traditional practices, even those with their basis in the Bible, such as not working on the sabbath.[11] With that background, there is no reason to assume that he ate lamb at the seder just because that was the traditional thing to do. If Jesus condemned animal sacrifice as sinful, as we have just seen that he did, it stands to reason that he would not sacrifice a lamb for the Passover seder.

* * *

The attitude of the early Jewish followers of Jesus toward animal sacrifice is reflected in Hebrews, an epistle written to convince Jews that Jesus was the messiah. In a lengthy passage devoted to the proposition that the blood of Jesus has replaced the blood of sacrificial animals as a means of expiating sin, the unknown Jewish Christian author observes that this was necessary because animal sacrifices had never been effective. If they had been, "would they not have ceased to be offered, because the worshippers, having once been cleansed, would no longer have had consciousness of sins?" (Hebrews 10:2) He continues with the blanket statement that "it is impossible for the blood of bulls and goats to take away sins" (Hebrews 10:4), and then quotes with approval Psalm 40:6–8 in the Septuagint version, which says, "SACRIFICE AND OFFERING YOU HAVE NOT DESIRED, BUT A BODY YOU HAVE PREPARED FOR ME. IN WHOLE BURNT OFFERINGS AND *SACRIFICES* FOR SIN YOU HAVE TAKEN NO PLEASURE."[12] (Hebrews 10:5–6)

Therefore, Choose Life

"See, I have set before thee this day life and good, and death and evil . . . Therefore, choose life." (Deuteronomy 30:15, 19, KJV) In regard to animal sacrifice, the prophets and Jesus chose life. In regard to biomedical research and product testing on animals, the Prime Directives summon us to do the same.

Notes

1. I have quoted the NIV here because the NASB says "loyalty" where most English Bibles say "mercy." The Septuagint says "mercy" (*eleos*), as does the Latin Vulgate (*misericordia*). In a margin note, the NASB gives "lovingkindness" as an alternative to "loyalty." In the Septuagint, this sentence appears as verse 7.

2. After the death of Solomon, the Jewish kingdom split into two separate states, Judah in the south and Israel in the north. "Ephraim" refers to the northern kingdom.

3. "Altar" by Howard Z. Cleveland, Th.D., in Tenney, pp. 31–32.

4. See, for example, Deuteronomy 12:5–6 and 1 Samuel 14:32–35.

5. Strong number 7306. See Strong, p. 1257, and Hebrew Dictionary section, p. 130. Wigram, *Hebrew Concordance*, p. 1160. Brown et al., p. 926.

6. No one knows what the Psalmist meant when he said, "My ears You have opened." The two most popular guesses are that God opened his ears so he could hear God's commands, and that God pierced his earlobe to insert an earring as a token that he was God's slave. This sentence does not appear in the Septuagint, which says instead, "A body You have prepared for me." No one knows what that means, either.

7. This incident is also described in Matthew 8:2–4 and Luke 5:12–14. I have followed Mark's version because it provides more detail and clearly states the sequence of events, which is essential for understanding what Jesus was saying.

8. The sacrifices for cured leprosy are described in Leviticus 14.

9. *The Gospel of the Ebionites,* in Barnstone, p. 338. For an insightful discussion of the Ebionites and their gospel, see Akers, 2000.

10. The Last Supper is described in Matthew 26:17–30, Mark 14:12–26, Luke 22:7–39, and John 13:1–18:1. John contradicts the other three gospels by specifically denying that it was a seder, stating that it took place before Passover began (13:1). If John is correct, there is no issue at all. Paul briefly describes the Last Supper in 1 Corinthians 11:23–25.

11. E.g., Matthew 12:1–8 and John 9:1–16.

12. Earlier in this chapter, I quoted the same passage from Psalms following the standard Hebrew version, which is known as the Masoretic text, that appears in most of our English Bibles.

9: They Shall Be Yours for Food

In the Garden of Eden, God instructed Adam and Eve to follow not simply a vegetarian but a vegan diet, one that takes nothing from any living soul: not her life, not her eggs, not her milk, and not her freedom and joy.

> Then God said, "Behold, I have given you every plant yielding seed that is on the surface of the earth, and every tree which has fruit yielding seed; it shall be food for you; and to every beast of the earth and to every bird of the sky and to every thing that moves on the earth which has life [every *nephesh chayah*, every "living soul"], *I have given* every green plant for food'; and it was so. God saw all that He had made, and behold, it was very good." (Genesis 1:29–31)

It was very good because there was no violence. No living soul harmed any other living soul. All of God's children lived together in peace.

With the expulsion from the Garden of Eden, that came to an end. Animals began to kill and eat one another. Human beings began to kill and eat animals and to kill one another in feuds and wars. Violence, suffering, and death entered the world. And so, the Bible teaches, it will remain until the Garden of

Eden is recreated in the Peaceable Kingdom. But one thing did
not change with the expulsion from the Garden. God's
command that humankind maintain a vegan diet stayed in effect
until after the flood, although over time it was increasingly
disobeyed.

* * *

Genesis tells us that after Noah and his family emerged from the
ark,

> God blessed Noah and his sons and said to them, "Be
> fruitful and multiply; and fill the earth. The fear of you
> and the terror of you will be on every beast of the earth
> and on every bird of the sky; with everything that creeps
> on the ground, and all the fish of the sea, into your hand
> they are given. Every moving thing that is alive shall be
> food for you; I give all to you as *I gave* the green plant."
> (Genesis 9:1–3)

Before going on, we should note that this passage confirms that
God did mandate a strict vegan diet in the Garden of Eden.
Some commentators have tried to claim that Genesis 1:28–31
does not say that green plants should be humankind's *only* food,
but simply that they are there to be used as food, and that these
verses do not prohibit eating animal flesh as well. But that claim
cannot be maintained in the light of "I give you them all, as *I
gave* the green plant," which makes clear that up until this point
God's command to humankind had been to eat only plants—
even though that command may have been much violated.

   The first question we have to ask about this passage is, Does
it conform to the Prime Directives? Is it consistent with loving
God with all our heart, all our soul, and all our might, and with

loving our neighbors as ourselves? I believe that the answer is a firm No. We cannot love God by making "the fear and terror" of us fall upon God's children. And we do not love our neighbors by terrorizing and killing them to satisfy our appetites. Looking to the Golden Rule of Hillel and Jesus, we would not want others to kill us for food—especially food they did not need to live long, healthy lives—and so we should not kill them. It is that simple. When a bear, a lion, or a tiger kills a single human being, there is universal outrage. The animal is labeled "vicious," "savage," or, most horrifying of all, "a man eater." And yet every day, in the United States alone, we kill twenty-five million animals for food. That is the equivalent of two and a half holocausts a day in Singer's eternal Treblinka, simply because we enjoy the taste and texture of their flesh or mistakenly think that our health depends upon killing and eating them. Animal agriculture and slaughter are atrocities of such grand magnitude that nothing else in history can approach them. They cannot be reconciled with the Prime Directives.

The next question we have to ask is, When we slaughter animals for food, are we exercising the dominion of love? Are we living as the image of God, whose nature is love and compassion? Again, I believe the answer is a firm No. Love does not kill casually for selfish motives, and compassion does not turn a blind eye to the suffering of others. And so, since these verses fail the test of the Prime Directives and lead us away from the dominion of love and away from a life reflecting the image of God, I believe that they are line noise and not God's authentic inspiration.

Eating is one of our basic physical and psychological drives. And one of our greatest weaknesses is that we want to eat anything and everything that tastes good. Every day, vast numbers of people ruin their physical health because they eat things that are not good for their bodies. They know better, but they can't resist the temptation; the urge of appetite is too strong. We should not be surprised that people will also ruin their moral and spiritual health by eating things that are not good for their souls. Nor should we be surprised that the urge of appetite was so strong that the writer of this passage in Genesis mistook it for the voice of God. The claim that God rescinded the original injunction to keep a vegan diet and gave us approval to eat meat may be, in its consequences, the most tragic burst of static to break into the Bible narratives; but it is not hard to understand how the still, small voice of veganism could be drowned out by the tumult of the meat eating that the Israelites found all around them. In the modern era, it is still being drowned out in synagogues and churches all around us.

In the previous chapter, we saw that several of the prophets and one of the Psalmists condemned animal sacrifice. Following the exodus and during the conquest of Israel, Jews were forbidden to eat meat from an animal who had not been slaughtered at an altar.[1] The only meat that could be eaten was meat that had been offered as a sacrifice. Animal sacrifice and ritual slaughter (*shechitah*) were one and the same thing. When this restriction ceased to be honored we do not know; but as late as 70 CE, when the Temple was destroyed by the Romans, bringing animal sacrifice to an abrupt halt, the leading rabbis of the time debated whether Jews could continue to eat meat.[2] It seems likely that when the prophets condemned animal sacrifice they were also condemning meat eating.

An Alternative View

I have no doubt that the approval to eat meat after the flood is line noise that has overridden the genuine inspiration of the Bible. But for those who remain convinced that it reflects the authentic word of God, there is another way to look at it that is widely advocated within the Jewish and Christian vegetarian communities.

One of the most striking features of this permission to eat meat is that it is not a commandment. Nowhere does God say, "Thou shalt eat meat." Nor is it a recommendation. God does not even say, "Why don't you start eating meat? It tastes good." It is no more than what I called it: permission. Eating animal products is not presented here as any sort of religious requirement or virtuous act; it is simply—for the first time since creation—allowed. Many scholars, both Jewish and Christian, see in this permission a reluctant, even sorrowful, recognition by God that humanity was still too mired in ignorance and selfishness to live up to the ideal of the Peaceable Kingdom. A quick look at the setting will show why.

The Bible teaches that the flood was God's response to the growing wickedness of humanity. Almost from the beginning, humankind had abandoned the dominion of love for hatred and violence. Adam and Eve's son, Abel, killed a sheep for a sacrifice. In turn, his brother, Cain, killed Abel, jealous because he believed God had preferred Abel's offering to his own offering of vegetables and grain. From there, things went steadily downhill as humankind developed the arrogance, vices, and violent proclivities that we see all around us today. As I once heard a Methodist minister say from the pulpit, "Things on earth had got so bad that God decided to hose it down and start over." But God did not quite start over from scratch. God saved one human family and either two of every kind of animal or fourteen of some and two of others.[3] But in any event, after the water had subsided, the first thing Noah did when he came out of the ark was to slaughter an animal and offer him to God as a sacrifice.

How that must have saddened God. The family that God had spared from the flood, who would be the ancestors of all of humankind for all time to come, had learned nothing. When God said, "The fear of you and the terror of you will be on every beast of the earth and on every bird of the sky; with everything that creeps on the ground, and all of the fish of the sea, into your hand they are given," God was not commanding that it should be so, but acknowledging that humanity was still so mired in greed and violence that it could not be otherwise, a fact announced by the sacrifice that Noah had just offered. And when God said, "Every moving thing that is alive shall be for you; I give all to you, as *I gave* the green plant," that was not a divine blessing, but a concession to a human race that—driven by our peculiar blend of weakness and stubbornness—was still unwilling to practice the dominion of love and live in the image of God. In the words of Rabbi Shlomo Riskin, "Only after the flood, when God saw that man's instinct was deeply imbedded with a desire to kill, did He allow man to spill the blood of an animal and eat its flesh . . . It's a concession, not the ideal."[4]

Abraham Isaac Kook (1865–1935) was the first Ashkenazic chief rabbi of modern Israel prior to nationhood, and a leading twentieth-century exponent of Orthodox Judaism. His English translator and editor Ben Zion Bokser speaks of Rabbi Kook's "inclusion of animals in the fullest unfolding of morality. The universal man of the future, he believed, would abandon the eating of meat and return to a vegetarian diet, to which he had been confined before Adam's disobedience in eating the forbidden fruit. The permission to eat meat was a concession to man's moral weakness, but he would rise out of it when his spiritual development reached the level of true universality."[5]

Reverend J. R. Hyland makes this observation about the permission to eat meat: "This verse of scripture is a statement of fact: human beings will consume the flesh of other creatures . . . human chauvinism has prompted scholars to claim that it constitutes God's blessing on man turned carnivore. But the passage does not signify divine approval of what has taken place. It is not approval—it is acceptance of what has already happened."[6]

Sometimes I hear the objection that God would not make concessions of this sort to the stubbornness of humankind. But the Bible cites other instances of God doing precisely that. After the exodus, the people of Israel were governed by a theocracy; their leaders were men (and at least one woman, Deborah) known as "judges" who were believed to be favored by God. Eventually, the people grew tired of this arrangement and began clamoring to be ruled by a secular king just as their neighbors were. God tried to talk them out of it, but they persisted until finally God grudgingly relented. (1 Samuel 8:4–22) In the New Testament, Jesus describes divorce as a divine concession to the hardness of the human heart. (Matthew 19:8)

* * *

In the same passage in Genesis that allows the eating of meat, God put in place an absolute injunction against eating "flesh with its life, *that is*, its blood," still in it. (Genesis 9:4) As a reminder that by eating meat they were taking a life, and thereby failing to live up to the ideal of the Peaceable Kingdom, God required that the blood be drained from a slaughtered animal for all to see before his flesh could be eaten. As this is one the earliest Biblical foundations of the Jewish dietary code, some Jewish scholars, including Rabbi Kook, see in it a sign that the kosher laws are not a seal of divine approval on meat eating, but a reminder to humanity that when we kill to satisfy our appetites we sin. Of the commandment to pour out the blood of an animal killed by a hunter and cover it with earth (Leviticus 17:13), Rabbi Kook says, "This is the beginning of moral therapy . . . It means: Cover the blood! Hide your shame! These efforts will bear fruit, in the course of time people will be educated. The silent protest will in time be transformed into a mighty shout and it will triumph in its objective. The regulations of slaughter, in special prescriptions, to reduce the pain of the animal registers a reminder that we are not dealing with things outside the law, that they are not automatons devoid of life, but with living things . . . the rule to cover the blood extends the sway of 'You shall not murder' to the animal, and the prohibition against mixing meat and milk and the banning of linen and wool in a garment extends the injunctions 'You shall not rob' and 'You shall not oppress . . .' "[7] In Rabbi Kook's view, the kosher restrictions are God's reproach to a morally deficient humanity and a reminder that the absolute moral distinction between humankind and animals is our creation, not God's.

Rabbi Kook's point that "the rule to cover the blood extends the sway of 'You shall not murder' to the animal" becomes clearer when we realize that the word that the NASB, in common with most English Bibles, translates "life" is our old friend *nephesh*. The basic Hebrew word for "life" is *chayyim*, to which *chayah*, as in *nephesh chayah*, is related. The use of *nephesh* instead of *chayyim* in connection with blood indicates that the writer was not talking about life *per se*, but about the unique God-given vital essence of the individual animal. If translators were not so determined to deny souls to animals, they would say, "the *soul*, which is the blood," instead of "the *life*, which is the blood."

The fact is that the ancient Jews did not believe that "the blood is the life." Like other ancient peoples, they believed that the breath is the life. At creation, Adam became a living soul not when God put blood into his veins, but when God "breathed into his nostrils the breath of life." (Genesis 2:7) Reflecting this, the Hebrew word for "spirit" is *ruach*, which has the primary meanings of "breath" and "wind."[8] The Greek word for "spirit" is *pneuma*, which also means "breath" or "wind."[9] All living beings breathe, and when death comes, breathing stops. A common test for death in the ancient world was to hold a mirror over the mouth to see if it fogged. If it did not, breathing had ceased, and the person was dead. Blood might remain in the body after death, but never breath.

I believe that the ancient Jews associated blood with the soul because it was diffused throughout all the living tissue of the body. Tissue that had no blood, such as nails, hair, and calluses, was not alive. The blood was the physical medium through which the living soul infused the body; it was, so to speak, the carrier of the soul. Hunters were commanded to bury the blood of their prey to hide the shame of having taken a soul.

The flesh must never be eaten with the blood still in it because that would be symbolically eating the soul of the animal, even though in a literal sense that soul had departed with the breath. These requirements were a reminder that killing any living soul was a form of murder. In Rabbi Kook's phrase, these commandments extended *Thou shalt not kill* to all living beings. Sadly, the lesson has not been learned. Most observant Jews are content to follow the letter of the regulations, while Christians have jettisoned the kosher restraints entirely.

* * *

In the same passage in Genesis in which God granted the concession to eat meat—just a few verses farther on—God also made the covenant with the animals that we cited earlier: never again to destroy the world by water, never again to visit that kind of terror, suffering, and early death upon all living souls. Humankind might have so little concern for animals as to slaughter and eat them, but to God they were important enough to be partners and beneficiaries in a divine covenant, and God wanted to make sure that Noah and his family—and after them all of humankind—knew it.

An Unfamiliar Love

According to this alternative view, God has given humanity a high road and a low road, and the freedom to choose. And so the issue becomes, Why—even if it may be permitted—would anyone who is trying to reflect God's love and compassion onto the world want to eat meat, eggs, or dairy? As I have remarked before—and will continue to repeat because it is such a fundamental point and so widely ignored—the raising and slaughter of animals for food and fabric causes intense physical pain, emotional distress, and premature death to ten billion animals every year in the United States alone. This entire system of torment and death exists solely for those who consume animal products. If it were not for them, no animals would be confined on factory farms and no animals would be slaughtered. Not only does using animal products violate the Bible's Prime Directives, it violates universal concepts of simple human decency. Why would any person of good will—regardless of their religion—want to be responsible for so much innocent suffering and death? Why would anyone want to bear the moral burden of Isaac Bashevis Singer's eternal Treblinka?

In his story "The Slaughterer," Singer incarnates this burden in Yoineh Meir, a young man who had studied to follow his father and grandfather as the rabbi of the town of Kolomir in Eastern Europe. At the last minute, Yoineh lost the post as a result of community politics and as a kind of consolation prize was appointed Kolomir's ritual slaughterer. Not wanting to embark on a career of killing, he accepted the post only after a famous rabbi assured him that he would actually be liberating the souls of saints who had taken rebirth as animals to do penance for some small sin. But the brutal reality of slaughter was overwhelming, and soon Yoineh "felt as though he were immersed in blood and lymph. His ears were beset by the squawking of hens, the crowing of roosters, the gobbling of geese, the lowing of oxen, the mooing and bleating of calves and goats. . . The bodies refused to know any justification or excuse—every body resisted in its own fashion, tried to escape, and seemed to argue with the Creator to its last breath." Yoineh sought refuge in religious study and worship, but to no avail, "The smell of the slaughterhouse would not leave his nostrils." As the month of Elul, with its numerous Holy Days, approached, Yoineh was stricken by the thought of the animals who would be slaughtered for the celebrations. "Millions of fowl and cattle now alive were doomed to be killed. Yoineh Meir no longer slept at night. If he dozed off he was immediately beset by nightmares" of animals taking on human form while he was slaughtering them. "An unfamiliar love welled up in Yoineh Meir for all that crawls and files, breeds and swarms. Even the mice— was it their fault that they were mice? What wrong does a mouse do? All it wants is a crumb of bread or a bit of cheese." One day, overcome by visions of blood running from the sun and intestines, livers, and kidneys growing from trees, and believing himself to be pursued by the animals that he slaughtered, Yoineh Meir ran off into the woods. Three days later, his body was found in a nearby river, drowned. "Because it was the holiday season and there was danger that Kolomir might remain without meat, the community hastily dispatched two messengers to bring a new slaughterer."[10]

An acute moral crisis that affected the townspeople profoundly—for they had created it—was seen as simply a random episode of madness that had nothing to do with them— and certainly nothing to teach them. The slaughter of innocent animals was a matter of appetite and tradition, not love for God and neighbor. Yoineh Meir's "unfamiliar love" for all creatures had failed to touch them—just as it fails to touch most of us today.

Vegan Food from Heaven

A story from the exodus lends added credence to the idea that
meat eating was a reluctant concession by God to the lust and
stubbornness of humankind. Shortly after escaping from Egypt
into the Sinai desert, the Israelites began complaining loudly
about not having enough to eat. "Would that we had died by the
LORD'S hand in the land of Egypt," they complained to Moses,
"When we sat by the pots of meat, when we ate bread to the full;
for you have brought us out into this wilderness to kill this
whole assembly with hunger." (Exodus 16:3) To put an end to
their constant griping, Moses asked God to give them food in
addition to what they were able to gather in the desert.

In response to Moses' plea, God provided the Israelites with
a mysterious food called manna. Exactly what manna was, no
one knows, but the Bible describes it as forming on the ground
with the dew and also vanishing with the dew unless it was
protected from sunlight. It looked like coriander seeds, had the
color of gum resin, and tasted like cakes dipped in honey. Even
though it was tasty, nutritious, and plentiful, the Israelites soon
tired of a steady diet of manna, and again took up their cry for
meat. Exasperated, Moses vented his frustration to God.
"Haven't I always done everything you wanted? So why have you
stuck me with this grief? What did I do to deserve being put in
charge of this crew? Am I their mother? Did I bring them into
the world? So why do I have to put up with their everlasting
whining and their 'Give us meat?' This is more than I can take!
Why don't you just kill me now and put me out of my misery?"
(Numbers 11:11-15, condensed and paraphrased)

To teach the Israelites a lesson, God told them, "Consecrate
yourselves for tomorrow, and you shall eat meat; for you have
wept in the ears of the LORD, saying, 'Oh that someone would
give us meat to eat! For we were well-off in Egypt.' Therefore,
the LORD will give you meat and you shall eat. You shall eat, not

one day, nor two days, nor five days, nor ten days, nor twenty days, but a whole month, until it comes out of your nostrils and becomes loathsome to you; because you have rejected the LORD who is among you and have wept before Him, saying, 'Why did we ever leave Egypt?' " (Numbers 11:18–20)

God could have given the Israelites any type of food at all, but God did not want them to eat meat, and so they were provided with vegan food in the form of manna. It was plentiful, tasty, and easy to prepare. But the people were not satisfied with it. They set up a cry for meat and began talking of their slavery in Egypt as the good old days. And so, according to the story, God decided to teach them a lesson. In response to their demand for meat, God sent an enormous flock of quail who settled in all around the camp so that the people were able to catch them, kill them, and cook them. But "While the meat was still between their teeth, before it was chewed, the anger of the LORD was kindled against the people, and the LORD struck the people with a very severe plague. So the name of that place was called Kibroth-hattaavah" because there they buried the people who had been greedy." (Numbers 11:33–34) In recounting the flight from Egypt, Exodus also reports the arrival of the quail, but delicately omits to mention God's anger at the Israelites for wanting meat or the fact that eating the quail caused a plague. In fact, the story is so distasteful to the author that he fails even to mention that the Israelites ate the quail. (Exodus 16:11–13) To the writer of this passage in Numbers, meat eating was a rebellion against God that needed to be remembered by future generations. The teller of the same story in Exodus was so horrified that he chose to look the other way.

In the Den of Iniquity

One of the most impressive testimonials you will ever find to the health benefits of a vegan diet is given in the book of Daniel.

When the Babylonians conquered Judah in 605 BCE, they took a
group of young Jewish men from aristocratic families back to
Babylon to be educated in the royal palace and enrolled in the
upper levels of the Babylonian civil service. One of these young
Jewish nobles, Daniel, along with three of his companions,
"made up his mind that he would not defile himself with the
king's choice food or with the wine which he drank; so he sought
permission from the commander of the officials that he might not
defile himself." (Daniel 1:8) The commander objected that if
their health suffered as a result of not following the royal diet,
the king would blame him. Daniel's rejoinder was "Please test
your servants for ten days, and let us be given some vegetables to
eat and water to drink. Then let our appearance be observed in
your presence and the appearance of the youths who are eating
the king's choice food; and deal with your servants according to
what you see." (Daniel 1:12–13) "At the end of ten days," we are
told, "their appearance seemed better and they were fatter than
all the youths who had been eating the king's choice food."
(Daniel 1:15) There were no further objections to their vegan
diet.

Years later, Daniel, who had risen high in the king's service
and gained a reputation as a seer, entered what we would call a
three-week retreat in search of a vision. "I did not eat any tasty
food, nor did meat or wine enter my mouth, nor did I use any
ointment at all until the entire three weeks were completed."
(Daniel 10:3) Clearly, by this time Daniel was no longer a vegetarian. Perhaps the mature courtier was less strict than the
young exile had been. Time, power, and privilege have a way of
eroding even the strongest principles. More likely, his youthful
objection to the king's food had been that it was not kosher and
had been dedicated as an offering to pagan deities, an almost
universal practice in the ancient world. Now, as a trusted palace
official with the king's permission to practice Judaism, Daniel

would have no difficulty arranging for kosher food that had not been offered to other gods. In any event, Daniel appears to have been a vegetarian only when faced with extraordinary circumstances.

A Mighty Hunter before the Lord

Historically, hunting is linked to the eating of animal flesh. The hunter's forays into the forest yielded food for his family or his village. In the industrialized world, this is no longer the case. Hunters today may eat what they kill, but they do not kill in order to eat. Modern hunters kill for pleasure—whether it be the pleasure of the pursuit, the pleasure of a fantasy in which they imagine themselves to be intrepid frontiersmen, the pleasure they find in the taste of the meat, or the rush that some men get when they squeeze the trigger and exercise the power of life and death.

Unlike Judaism, which disapproves of sport hunting,[12] most Christian denominations accept it as a legitimate pastime. Several years ago, the Saint Paul Pioneer Press carried an article describing a group of Roman Catholic priests who owned a hunting lodge in Michigan, where they went every fall to hunt deer.[13] One of the priests posed for the camera holding a compound bow and wearing his clerical collar with his hunting camouflage. In the article, he treated killing animals for sport as a joke. "Oh, of course, we pray for deer," he told the reporter. "Not only deer, but big deer."

Among evangelical Christians, hunting is sometimes treated as a form of Christian ministry. Alabama boasts a "Coon Hunt for Christ," there is a Christian Bowhunters Association, and a Maryland-based group, "Farmers and Hunters Feeding the Hungry," calls itself a "faith-based venison ministry."

This supposed association between hunting and piety is nowhere to be found in the Bible, which mentions very few hunters. The first is Nimrod, a great-grandson of Noah, who is described as "a mighty hunter before the LORD." (Genesis 10:9) Among Christians, this is generally taken to indicate divine approval of hunting, but the Jewish tradition interprets it differently. Nimrod was the king of Babel (Genesis 10:10), and by flaunting in God's face his wanton killing of God's creatures, Nimrod displayed the same impious arrogance that led him to try to build a tower to heaven (Genesis 11:1–9). On this reading, being called "a mighty hunter before the LORD" is not praise, but condemnation for showing disrespect to the Creator by failing to respect creation.

Another Biblical hunter was Esau, son of Isaac, grandson of Abraham, and twin brother of Jacob. "When the boys grew up, Esau became a skillful hunter, a man of the field, but Jacob was a peaceful man, living in tents." (Genesis 25:27) It was Jacob, the man who did not base his life on violence against animals, who became the ancestor of the people of Israel, not Esau the hunter. The prophet Malachi describes God's attitude toward the two brothers this way. " '*Was* not Esau Jacob's brother?' declares the LORD. 'Yet I have loved Jacob; but I have hated Esau, and I have made his mountains a desolation and *appointed* his inheritance for the jackals of the wilderness.' " (Malachi 1:2–3) According to the prophet, God blessed Jacob, the man of peace, and his descendants after him, but cursed Esau, the skillful hunter, and those who descended from him. Isaac, who was also a hunter, had wanted the blessing to rest upon Esau, and not upon Jacob, but that was not to be. Genesis attributes this to the machinations of Rebecca, the twins' mother,[14] but according to Malachi, it was the will of God.

Earlier in this chapter, we quoted Leviticus 17:13, which says that when a hunter kills an animal, "he shall pour out its blood and cover it with earth," and we saw that that Rabbi Kook interpreted this commandment to mean that hunting was a shameful activity, a form of murder.

And so it is. Hunters shoot unsuspecting animals from ambush, or shoot them in the back as they flee in terror for their lives. They put out food and kill them as they eat. People who do to dogs and cats what hunters do to deer and mourning doves are prosecuted for animal cruelty. But animals in the wild are just as capable of suffering fear and pain as are our companions. What is cruel to one is cruel to the other. Hunting is legalized cruelty to animals. It cannot be reconciled with the Prime Directives.

Notes

1. See, for example, 1 Samuel 14:31–35. Seeing his tired and hungry troops about to slaughter and eat sheep and cattle that they had taken as the spoils of war, Saul built an emergency altar on the spot to keep them from committing blasphemy.
2. "The Dietary Laws as an Atonement for Flesh Eating" by Louis A. Berman, in Kalechofsky, 1992, p.151.
3. Compare Genesis 6:19–20 with Genesis 7:2–3.
4. "Compassion or Concession" by Rabbi Shlomo Riskin, in Kalechofsky, 1992, p. 45.
5. Kook, p. 249
6. Hyland, p. 26.
7. Kook, pp. 319, 321.
8. Strong number 7307. Brown et al., p. 924.
9. Strong number 4151. Thayer, p. 520.
10. Isaac Bashevis Singer, pp. 207–216.
11. "Graves of lust."
12. See Schwartz, p. 25.
13. "The Call of the Mild" by Bob Gwizdz of Newhouse News Service in the *Saint Paul Pioneer Press*, November 17, 1996.
14. See Genesis 27.

10: Fish Stories

Not long ago, People for the Ethical Treatment of Animals (PETA) proclaimed that "Jesus was a vegetarian," and began putting up billboards showing the image from the Shroud of Turin with an invitation to "Make a Lasting Impression" by becoming vegetarian. PETA made a lasting impression on popular Catholic writer Kevin Orlin Johnson, author of a book about the Shroud, who felt compelled to attack PETA's claim in no uncertain terms. According to a press release, Dr. Johnson said, "The Gospels—the most detailed records we have—say explicitly that he ate fish and lamb regularly." The item concludes by telling us that "Johnson says he doesn't know how the group could make their claim when the Gospel makes such a point of Jesus's use of animal food. 'I guess they didn't read it,' he says.'"

Dr. Johnson's assertions are so patently false that one has to wonder whether *he* has read the gospels. It is hard to understand how someone who makes a career of being an authority on Christianity would have the temerity to make such claims. But sadly, his statement is only too typical of what most Christians hear from their clergy and scholars, people who ought to know better because they have been intensively trained in New Testament studies. That they don't know better testifies to the power of prejudice to blind even people who are intelligent and well educated. And there is no prejudice more deeply engrained in our society than meat eating.

Contrary to Johnson's claim, as we saw in the previous chapter, *the Bible never says that Jesus ate lamb on any occasion, including the Last Supper.* In fact, *the Bible never suggests that Jesus ever consumed any kind of animal product except fish.* It does say that he ate fish, but only once, after his resurrection, when he took a small bite to prove to his disciples that he was truly resurrected and not merely a ghost. Nowhere do the gospels say that fish was part of Jesus' normal diet. Nevertheless, they do convey the impression of a strong connection between Jesus and fish used for food. So let's take a closer look at what that impression is based on.

Fishers of Men and Women

Jesus' earliest recorded encounter with fish—or at least with fishers—took place at the beginning of his ministry, when he was recruiting his first disciples.

> Now as Jesus was walking by the Sea of Galilee, He saw two brothers, Simon who was called Peter, and Andrew his brother, casting a net into the sea; for they were fishermen. And He said to them, "Follow Me, and I will make you fishers of men."[12] Immediately they left their nets and followed Him. Going on from there He saw two other brothers, James the *son* of Zebedee, and John his brother, in the boat with Zebedee their father, mending their nets; and He called them. Immediately, they left the boat and their father, and followed Him. (Matthew 4:18–22)

Mark and Luke also tell this story (Mark 1:16–20, Luke 5:1–11). Mark agrees with Matthew in laying great stress on the

immediacy with which the four brothers left their work—Simon
and Andrew their fishing, James and John mending their nets—
"immediately they left their nets," "immediately He called them;
and they left their father Zebedee in the boat." Luke contradicts
Matthew and Mark by having Jesus hang around to help them
with their fishing. In Luke, Jesus gets into Simon's boat, and tells
him to push out into deep water and lower his nets. Simon
objects that they have been fishing all night with no luck, but he
does as Jesus says and hauls in so many fish that the net begins
to split. He signals to James and John to come alongside, and
together they load so many fish that both boats are in danger of
sinking. This miraculous catch frightens Simon, who falls at
Jesus' feet and begs, "Go away from me, Lord, for I am a sinful
man, O Lord!" But Jesus tells him not to be afraid: " 'From now
on you will be catching men.' When they had brought their
boats to land, they left everything and followed him."

Both versions of this story cannot be right. John Mark, the
primary author of the gospel of Mark, was Simon Peter's inter-
preter when the apostle preached to Greek-speaking audiences,
and his gospel represents the recollections of Peter.[3] Matthew
was one of the original Twelve, and although he was not present
at this scene, he would have had ample opportunity to hear
Andrew, Peter, James, and John reminisce. Beyond that, his
gospel incorporates a great deal of material from Mark, even to
using the same phrasing, and this episode seems to fall into that
category. By contrast, Luke was a gentile who never met Jesus
and probably did not even speak Aramaic, the language spoken
by Jesus and his disciples. A travelling companion of Paul,[4] Luke
likely met Peter but had only slight contact with him, since Peter
and Paul spent little time together and were not always on
friendly terms.[5] Therefore, as he tells us in the introduction to
his gospel, Luke had to rely on secondhand sources for his information. Matthew and Mark—who got their version directly

from the participants—give the simpler, more straightforward account. Clearly, theirs is the original. Luke has grafted onto their memory a miraculous folk legend that he found in an unknown source. If Luke's miracle had actually taken place, and had made the deep impression on Simon Peter that Luke tells us it did, Peter would certainly have recounted it when he told the story, and Mark would have included it in his gospel. Since he did not, we can safely conclude that Jesus did not use the miraculous powers given him by God to kill two boatloads of fish.

* * *

Students of the Bible have long puzzled over the meaning of "I will make you fishers of men." Fish are caught for their death, while the men and women would be "fished" for their salvation. One possibility is that the phrase was simply a cliché. In the fifth century BCE, the historian Timon of Athens disparagingly characterized the proselytizing of the Greek philosopher and religious leader Pythagoras as "fishing for men," and Timon's colorful image may have passed into common usage.[6]

The other possibility, which seems more likely, is that Jesus was calling the brothers to turn their own lives around by abandoning the sinful occupation of killing God's creatures and embarking on a vocation of introducing men and women to salvation. "Stop bringing death to God's children," Jesus may have been saying, "And bring eternal life to men and women instead." The suddenness with which the fishermen deserted their old profession and embraced the new lends force to this notion. The two sets of brothers give the impression of men who were filled with disgust at their old lives and could not wait to leave them behind.

When they became disciples of Jesus, Andrew, Peter, James, and John gave up fishing forever. The New Testament tells of only one occasion on which they reverted to their old way of life, a one-night stand as it were, immediately following the crucifixion, after which they never fished again. (John 21) We will discuss this incident in detail later in this chapter.

It is often claimed that Jesus' choice of four commercial fishers to be his disciples shows that he approved of killing and eating animals; but for Andrew and Simon, James and John, becoming disciples of Jesus required giving up fishing. Religious conversion often involves abandoning a way of life that is now recognized as sinful. And often, men and women who were the greatest sinners go on to become the greatest saints. That is the way I believe it was with Simon Peter, his brother Andrew, and the sons of Zebedee.

Loaves and Fishes

The gospels record two occasions on which Jesus miraculously fed large crowds of people with small quantities of bread and fish. The first, known as the Feeding of the Five Thousand, is described in Matthew 14:14–21, Mark 6:34–44, Luke 9:11–17, and John 6:3–13. The details vary, but in all four versions, the story is essentially the same. According to John, Jesus had been addressing a large crowd on a hillside in Galilee. Late in the afternoon, near the end of a long day, he asked his disciples where they could buy bread to feed the people. Philip answered that enough bread to feed that many people would cost more than they could afford. Andrew piped up that a small boy had brought a lunch of five barley rolls and two "delicacies," a word which requires some explanation.

In the ancient world, the average person ate a grain-based diet. Some form of bread was the main course, and often the only course, at every meal. In an age without refrigeration and with stark divisions between rich and poor, only the well to do could afford meat or fresh vegetables on a regular basis. As a consequence, almost anything served in addition to bread was considered a "delicacy," the Greek word for which is *opsarion*.[7] An *opsarion* could be animal or vegetable, and the term encompassed all kinds of meat, including fish. Some scholars have suggested that since John uses the word *opsarion* here, the food in question may not have been fish, but some kind of vegetable "delicacy" instead. This is possible, but Matthew, Mark, and Luke do not say *opsarion*; they use the Greek word for "fish," *ichthys*. Galilee was a commercial fishing center, and ordinary people would more likely have fish there than in most other places. Our English Bibles simply assume that fish is meant and translate *opsarion* as "fish"; they are probably correct.

In any event, Jesus told his disciples to seat the crowd on the grass and distribute the five loaves and two fishes. Miraculously, the little boy's lunch fed the entire crowd with twelve basketfuls left over.

The second story of Jesus feeding a large crowd on a small quantity of bread and fish, known as the Feeding of the Four Thousand, is found only in Matthew and Mark. Here Jesus fed four thousand people on seven rolls and "a few small fishes," with seven baskets of leftovers. (Matthew 15:32–38, Mark 8:1–9)

In *The Lost Religion of Jesus*, Keith Akers makes a strong case that the original story spoke only of Jesus multiplying loaves of bread. Early in the second century, he notes, some two hundred years before the earliest gospel manuscripts that have come down to us were created, the Christian theologian Irenaeus retold both of these stories. In his narratives, Irenaeus spoke only of bread and never mentioned fish, suggesting that in the gospel manuscripts he read, the fish were not mentioned.[8] Around the beginning of the fourth century, a North African Christian writer named Arnobius included the Feeding of the Five Thousand in a list of Jesus' miracles, and he also mentioned only bread.[9] Finally, in the fourth century, Eusebius of Caesarea, the premier historian of the early church, also told the story of the Feeding of the Five Thousand, and like his predecessors, Irenaeus and Arnobius, he too made no mention of the fish, limiting the miracle to multiplication of the bread.[10]

Akers further points out that on two occasions the gospels quote Jesus as reminding the disciples of both miracles and mentioning only the bread, not the fish. (Matthew 16:9–10, Mark 8:18–20) Based on this evidence, Akers concludes that "Most likely, later redactors added fish to the story when only bread was recorded in the original tradition . . ."[11] No doubt this was done to make the miracle more impressive. Fish, even dead fish, are more complex entities than loaves of bread and, presumably, harder to multiply.

But while negative evidence can be suggestive—in this case, I believe it is highly suggestive—it is not proof, and there is another way to look at this story. All four gospels lay great stress on the fact that Jesus and his disciples did not procure or prepare the fish. In fact, when Jesus and his disciple Philip discussed the possibility of buying food for the crowd, they spoke only of bread and never mentioned fish. On both occasions, the fish were caught, cooked, and brought to the gathering without Jesus' knowledge. Having decided that the crowd was too large to buy bread for, he had to find some other way to feed them or send them away to feed themselves. If he sent them away, some would probably have bought fish, which were readily available in the area surrounding the Sea of Galilee. But the miraculous multiplication of fish who were already dead involved no harm to any living being. It caused no suffering and no death. The lesson that we should take away from these stories may be that when circumstances force us to choose between two less than perfect alternatives, we should take the path that causes less suffering, even at the risk of being misunderstood.

A Fish Will Deliver the Money

Matthew tells a strange story of Peter being approached in Capernaum, his home town on the shore of the Sea of Galilee, by the collectors of a tax that Jews were required to pay for the support of the Temple. Peter went straight to Jesus, who told him to go down to the water, drop in a fishing line and pull up the first fish that he hooked. Inside the fish's mouth, Jesus told him, Peter would find a coin with which he could pay the tax for both of them. We are not told whether Peter did this, nor if he did, what the result was. (Matthew 17:24–27)

It is hard to know what to make of this tale, which appears only in Matthew and has the sound of a folk-legend. Throughout his ministry in Galilee, Jesus was supported financially by a group of well-to-do women who traveled with him and his disciples.[12] He had a treasurer, Judas Iscariot, who looked after the group's finances.[13] He and his disciples lived a simple lifestyle, and there is no hint in the gospels that they ever experienced financial hardship. It is difficult to see why he would have needed to send Simon Peter fishing for a miracle to pay the Temple tax.

On balance, I believe that the coin in the fish's mouth is a popular story that circulated in Galilee and at some point became embedded in Matthew's gospel.

A Snake for a Fish

While teaching his disciples one day, Jesus asked them, "What man is there among you who, when his son asks for a loaf, will give him a stone? Or if he asks for a fish, he will not give him a snake, will he? If you then, being evil, know how to give good gifts to your children, how much more will your Father who is in heaven give what is good to those who ask Him!" (Matthew 7:9–11) This saying is also reported in Luke 11:11–13, "Now suppose one of you fathers is asked by his son for a fish; he will not give him a snake instead of a fish, will he? Or *if* he is asked for an egg, he will not give him a scorpion, will he? If you then, being evil, know how to give good gifts to your children, how much more will *your* heavenly Father give the Holy Spirit to those who ask Him?" Luke's substitution of "the Holy Spirit" for Matthew's "what is good," tells us that this story underwent changes in the course of being passed on; and, in fact, some ancient manuscripts of Luke do not say "the Holy Spirit," but "a good gift," while others say "good things." Also, some of the ancient manuscripts of Luke include Matthew's phrase "a stone when he asks for bread," while others do not.[14]

Clearly, this teaching did not acquire a stable form until quite late, making it impossible to know precisely what Jesus said. Still, the reference to a fish occurs in all of the ancient manuscripts of both Matthew and Luke, and we have no convincing reason to discount it. Since he included it in the category of "good things," or "good gifts," this saying strongly suggests that Jesus approved of eating fish.

A Locked Room Mystery

According to Acts 1:3, Jesus remained on earth for forty days following his resurrection. During this time, he did not live with his disciples, as he had before the crucifixion, but made only a few brief visits to them, appearing suddenly and unpredictably and leaving the same way.

One of these appearances to a group of disciples is described in Luke 24:36–43. "While they were telling these things [the story of an earlier appearance of the risen Jesus to Simon Peter], He Himself stood in their midst and said to them, 'Peace be to you.' But they were startled and frightened and thought that they were seeing a spirit. And He said to them, 'Why are you troubled, and why do doubts arise in your hearts? See My hands and My feet, that it is I Myself; touch Me and see, for a spirit does not have flesh and bones as you see that I have. And when He had said this, He showed them His hands and His feet. While they still could not believe *it* because of their joy and amazement, He said to them, 'Have you anything here to eat?' They gave Him a piece of broiled fish; and He took it and ate *it* before them." *This is the only occasion on which the Bible tells us that Jesus ate fish. In fact, it is the only occasion on which it tells us that Jesus ate anything other than bread.* And even here, it does not say that Jesus ate fish because he was hungry or because fish was a regular part of his diet, but because he wanted to demonstrate that his body had actually risen from the dead. Ghosts can't eat.

It could be argued that the disciples would not have been eating fish if Jesus had taught that fish should not be eaten. That is a legitimate argument, but not necessarily correct. At least four of Jesus' closest followers had been commercial fishers before joining him, and as we shall see in a moment, following his crucifixion, they briefly reverted to their former lifestyle. According to John 21, the resurrected Jesus rebuked them sharply for their backsliding into a way of life that they had left behind to become his disciples. Eating fish could well have been another symptom of this same backsliding of which Jesus so strongly disapproved. Be that as it may, we have to note that Jesus did not rebuke them on this occasion.

* * *

This appearance is also described in John 20:19–20, with two important variations. "So when it was evening on that day, the first *day* of the week, and when the doors were shut where the disciples were for fear of the Jews, Jesus came and stood in their midst and said to them, 'Peace *be* with you.' And when He had said this, He showed them both His hands and His side. The disciples then rejoiced when they saw the Lord." Luke tells us that the disciples thought Jesus was a ghost, but John tells us why. Not only had they seen Jesus dead and buried, but he had just materialized inside a locked room, a detail that Luke omits. The second variation is that Luke tells us Jesus ate a piece of fish, while John does not.

We have already observed that the primary author of Luke was a gentile who came late upon the scene. By the time he wrote his gospel, he tells us that "Many have undertaken to compile an account of the things accomplished among us, just as they were handed down to us by those who from the beginning were eyewitnesses and servants of the word." (Luke 1:1–2) The works of these "many" were Luke's source documents, and his accounts are thus secondhand at best, and may sometimes be third- or fourth-hand. Besides Luke, there are only three other gospels in the Bible, Matthew, Mark, and John. Since three hardly qualifies as "many,"[15] Luke must have relied on other gospels that were never accepted into the Bible. We know that many such gospels were in circulation during the first three centuries CE, and a number of them still exist. Some contain interesting and instructive material that is certainly authentic, but most were excluded from the New Testament because they were so filled with stories of fantastic miracles that the church decided they were untrustworthy and did not represent either historical fact or authentic revelation. These are the gospels that Luke tells us he—in part—relied upon.

By contrast, the primary author of John was one of Jesus' closest followers. He refers to himself as "the disciple whom Jesus loved,"[16] which can hardly be an exaggeration, because while hanging on the cross, Jesus entrusted his mother to John's care.[17] John was certainly present in the locked room when Jesus appeared to his disciples. He was an eyewitness to what he describes. Therefore, John's version of what happened seems more to be trusted than Luke's. This suggests that the fish eating came from a legend created to reinforce the doctrine of the bodily resurrection. John omitted it because he had been there and knew it hadn't happened, while Luke included it because he had to rely on secondhand sources and sometimes had no way to distinguish between legend and fact.

Breakfast on the Beach

Jesus' last recorded encounter with fishers and fish contains clear echoes of the first, when he had called Simon and Andrew, James and John from their life of commercial fishing. According to the last chapter of John, some time after Jesus' appearance in the closed room, Simon Peter, Thomas, Nathaniel, James and John (the sons of Zebedee), and two other disciples who are not named left Jerusalem, where Jesus had been crucified, and returned to their home country of Galilee. At Peter's suggestion they all went out in a boat, fishing. This was not recreational fishing or fishing for their own food, but a return to commercial fishing. We know this, first, because the disciples fished with a net from a boat large enough to hold all eight of them. Then as now, nets were used for commercial fishing; personal fishing was done with a hook and line, as we saw in the story of the fish with a coin in his mouth. Second, they fished at night. In a hot climate and without refrigeration, fresh fish would have to be eaten within hours of being caught or they would go bad. Fish caught during the day would spoil before they could be gotten to market, sold, prepared, cooked, and eaten the next day; they would not last overnight. But fish caught at night, or in the dark of the morning, could be gotten to market in time to be served fresh for dinner that same day.

And this raises the question, Why did Jesus' disciples return to commercial fishing? The answer is that with the death of Jesus, their ministry had collapsed. According to John, they knew that Jesus had risen from the dead, because they had seen him, but for all practical purposes, he had left them. He was not living with them, he was not preaching and teaching and healing the sick. He would occasionally—and unpredictably—make brief, mysterious visits, after which he would vanish again. They felt abandoned, they had no idea what they were supposed to do now, and they became discouraged. To them it looked like their mission was over, and so they decided to return to the only other life they knew. Disheartened, they went back to Galilee and resumed commercial fishing.

Just as in Luke's version of Simon Peter and Andrew's encounter with Jesus at the beginning of his ministry, the disciples had been fishing all night and caught nothing. When dawn came, they saw Jesus standing on the shore—about a hundred yards away—but they did not recognize him. He called to them to cast their net over the starboard side of the ship. They did, and just as Luke tells us had occurred on the first occasion, the net was so filled with fish that they could hardly haul it in. At this point, "the disciple whom Jesus loved" and Simon Peter realized that it was Jesus, and they made for shore, Simon impulsively jumping in and swimming. When they got ashore, they found Jesus cooking fish and toasting bread over a charcoal fire. He gave them the bread and fish to eat, but John does not tell us whether Jesus ate any himself.

After the disciples had eaten, Jesus got down to business. Turning to Simon Peter, he said, "Simon, *son* of John, do you love me more than these?" (John 21:15) And here we encounter a problem of interpretation. What exactly did Jesus mean by "more than these?" The text gives us no clue, but the editors of the NIV Study Bible speculate that Jesus' question could mean any of three things: First, it might mean, "Do you love me more than you love these other disciples?" Second, "Do you love me more than these other disciples love me?" and finally, "Do you love me more than you love these things?" meaning the fishing equipment.[18] Since John's Greek word *touton*, "these," could be either masculine or neuter, all three of the NIV commentators' options are grammatically possible. We shall have to look at the logic of the situation to see which is most likely.

Jesus had no reason to ask if Simon loved him more than Simon loved the other disciples. He had always been Jesus' most fiercely loyal follower, which was why Jesus had nicknamed him Peter, "Rock," in the first place—which rules out the NIV's first option. As for the second option, it seems out of character for Jesus—who always stressed to his disciples the importance of humility and self-effacement —to force Peter to declare in front of other disciples that he was superior to them in his love for Jesus. On two separate occasions in the recent past, Jesus had chastised the disciples for competing among themselves for leadership roles, telling them sharply, "Whoever wishes to become great among you shall be slave of all." (Mark 10:35–45, John 13:3–17) And so, we can safely rule out option two as well. Turning to the NIV's third option—that "these" should really be translated "these things," and refers to the fishing gear—the critical point is that Jesus had originally called Simon from a life of commercial fishing to a life of discipleship. Now, Jesus found Simon abandoning his calling to go back to fishing. He had a very good reason to ask if Simon loved his fishing gear more than he loved Jesus.

When Simon answered that he loved Jesus more, Jesus said, "Then feed my lambs." Twice more, Jesus repeated the question, twice more he received the same answer, and both times he told Simon, "Feed my sheep." Once again, as he had done at the beginning of his ministry, Jesus was calling Simon Peter from a life of commercial fishing to a life of spreading the gospel. And by repeating the question three times, he was publicly chiding Peter for how quickly he had slipped back into his old way of life. This time the message sank in, and we never again hear of

Simon Peter, or any disciple, fishing. What we do not know, because the gospels do not tell us, is whether Jesus wanted his disciples to abandon fishing because it is cruel or because it was a distraction from spreading the gospel. What we do know is that he insisted that they choose between fishing and preaching. They could not do both. And that being the case, the fact that four of Jesus' disciples had been commercial fishers cannot be used as evidence that Jesus approved of fishing.

*　*　*

Did Jesus really cook fish for his disciples' breakfast at the same time that he directed Simon Peter to give up fishing forever and devote himself to teaching the gospel? Portions of the story seem so reminiscent of Luke's version of the first calling of Simon and Andrew, James, and John that we have to wonder if the popular legend that Luke inserted near the beginning of his gospel may not have found its way into the end of John's. It seems likely, but there is no way to be certain. In the case of ethical teachings, we can test Biblical passages against the Prime Directives. But in the case of factual claims, we have no such touchstone.

And so, after closely examining all of the New Testament passages connecting Jesus with fish and fishers, we are back where we started. The gospels never say that Jesus ate fish as part of his regular diet. They never say that he ate fish at all except on one occasion after the resurrection when he is said to have eaten a single morsel to prove that he was present in his physical body, but even that meager claim seems not to have been part of the original story. And yet we still carry away the sense of an association between Jesus and fish used for food. Even if the credibility of each specific story can be legitimately brought into question, we have to wonder why all of these stories involve fish and not any other kind of meat. It could simply be that fish were plentiful and popular in Galilee and lent themselves to legend. Or it could have been known that Jesus ate no animal products except fish, so that stories linking him to fish would be believed while stories connecting him to other kinds of meat would not. In the final analysis, on the basis of the Biblical record, we cannot state with certainty that Jesus disapproved of eating fish. But the case that he did approve of eating fish is far weaker than it is usually made out to be. Historically, the question cannot be settled. The evidence does not exist.

Since there is no clear example to follow, Christians must be guided by Jesus' teaching, which we will examine in the following chapters. As we do so, keep in mind that suffocation is a terrifying way to die. All of us have experienced moments when we had something caught in our throats and could not get our breath. It is a frightening experience and one that gives us some intimation of what it must be like to drown. Likewise, the frantic, desperate flailing of fish kidnapped and imprisoned in the air communicates their terror in a way that is unmistakable. But there is one difference between us: trapped in the air, fish drown more slowly than we do trapped under water. Their panic is stretched out over a longer time. The end of their agony does not come quickly. In commercial fishing, the horror is compounded as thousands of fish are dumped together into huge containers to die buried beneath an enormous pile of their fellows, a mountain of fear, suffering, and lingering death. There is no way that catching or eating fish can be reconciled with Jesus' gospel of mercy.

Notes

1. "Jesus Was No Vegetarian, Author Says; Animal Rights Campaign Ignores Gospel Accounts of Christ's Diet," press release issued by Pegasus Press and carried by PRNewswire on October 4, 2000.

2. The Greek word that the NASB translates "men" is *anthropos*, which means "human being," regardless of gender.

3. Eusebius, *History of the Church*, 3.39.

4. Colossians 4:14, 2 Timothy 4:11, and Philemon 24.

5. See Galatians 2:11–14. Jesus had nicknamed Simon "the Rock" (Matthew 16:18), which in Aramaic is *kepha*. Paul has transliterated this nickname into Greek as *Kephas*, which is traditionally rendered into English as "Cephas." Most New Testament writers chose instead to translate Simon's nickname into Greek as *Petros*, meaning "Rock," which comes into English as "Peter."

6. Durant, p. 163. For Pythagoras, see Chapter 14, note 14.

7. Strong number 3795. See *Strong's Concordance*, "Greek Dictionary of the New Testament," p. 65. See also Thayer, p. 471.

8. Akers, 2000, p. 126.

9. Ibid.

10. Ibid.

11. Akers, 2000, p. 127.

12. Luke 8:1–3.

13. John 13:29.

14. Luke 11:11–13, New English Bible, main text and note *d*.

15. Luke's Greek word is *polloi*, which implies quite a large number, not simply a few. When used of people, it means a "crowd," a "mob," or the "masses." Strong number 4183. (Singular *polus*) See Thayer, p. 529.

16. For example, in John 19:26 and 20:2. For identification of "the disciple whom Jesus loved" as the author of the gospel of John, see John 21:20–24.

17. John 19:25–27.

18. NIV Study Bible, p. 1635.

11: What Did Jesus Eat?

A s we have seen, other than one morsel of fish, the New
Testament never claims that Jesus ate or drank any kind of
animal product. On the other hand, it never explicitly says that
he did not. Contrary to Dr. Johnson's claim, we do not know, on
the basis of direct evidence, whether Jesus was a vegetarian. And
so, in the absence of direct Biblical testimony, we have to turn to
the indirect evidence.

What Goes into Your Mouth

The most quoted saying of Jesus on the subject of food is found
in Matthew 15:1–20. A group of Pharisee scholars from Jerusalem
challenged Jesus because he and his disciples did not wash their
hands before meals in the manner that they believed was
required by Jewish dietary law. Jesus responded by accusing the
Pharisees of a much more serious violation of the law of Moses,
a scheme by which people could refuse to support their elderly
parents by bequeathing their estates to the Temple and claiming
that money spent on their parents would diminish the estate and
amount to a misappropriation of money promised to God. In
Jesus' view, this violated the commandment to honor one's
father and mother. "After Jesus called the crowd to Him, He said
to them, 'Hear and understand. *It is* not what enters into the
mouth *that* defiles the man, but what proceeds out of the mouth,

this defiles the man.' " Later, in response to a question by Simon Peter, Jesus explained what he meant: ". . . everything that goes into the mouth passes into the stomach and is thrown out into the latrine. But the things that proceed out of the mouth come from the heart,[1] and those defile the man. For out of the heart come evil thoughts, murders, adulteries, fornications, thefts, false witness, slanders. These are the things which defile the man; but to eat with unwashed hands does not defile the man."

This passage, or at least the phrase, "It is not what enters the mouth that defiles the man, but what proceeds out of the mouth, this defiles the man," is often cited by defenders of meat eating as a direct statement by Jesus that it is morally permissible to eat whatever you want, including meat. But this cannot be so, because if it were, Jesus would be endorsing cannibalism. And yet, I have never met a Christian who believed that a person would not be "defiled" by eating human flesh. But if eating human flesh is wrong despite Jesus' blanket statement, why not animal flesh as well? We can either take Jesus' statement at face value, or not. But if we do, we have to accept that eating a human "drumstick" would not defile the one who ate it. Otherwise, we have look more closely at the context to see what Jesus meant.

As we can see from the second portion that I quoted, Jesus was not talking about what we eat at all, but about how we eat it. Jesus had not been accused of eating meat; he had not even been accused of eating unkosher meat. He had been accused of not washing his hands properly before eating. And that is the question to which he was responding. "But to eat with unwashed hands," Jesus said, "does not defile the man." Jesus' point was that right and wrong do not reside in rituals such as washing your hands before meals, but in our motives and in how we treat others.

When Jesus said that what goes into your mouth does not defile you, that is literally true. The sin in eating meat does not reside in the eating, but in the imprisonment and killing that are necessary to obtain the meat. If you came across an animal—or a human being—who had died of natural causes, skinned and dressed him, cooked and ate his flesh, that might be esthetically revolting and hygienically unsafe, but it would not be immoral, because you did not cause a living being to suffer or die. On the other hand, when you go into a restaurant and order spaghetti and meat sauce, that is a profoundly immoral act because you are participating in the imprisonment, torture, and murder of the animal whose flesh is in the sauce. Worse still, you are supporting in the most important way—with your money—the entire system of factory farms and slaughterhouses that provide our meat. You are sponsoring death camps for the weakest of God's children. You become a patron of the eternal Treblinka. You violate both of the Prime Directives.

Further evidence that Jesus did not intend this statement to justify meat eating is found in the tenth chapter of Acts, a passage that we shall consider in detail a bit farther on. Simon Peter had a vision of animals, both kosher and unkosher, being lowered from heaven in a blanket while a heavenly voice told him to kill and eat them. Peter refused on the grounds that he had never eaten anything "unclean." Peter had been present when Jesus gave his teaching about what goes into one's mouth. It had been Peter who asked the question that Jesus answered by saying, "but to eat without first washing his hands, that cannot defile him." Obviously, Peter had not understood Jesus' saying to mean that we cannot sin by our choice of food. Otherwise, he would not have objected to the heavenly voice that he had never eaten anything unclean.

Once, when I was about ten years old, my grandmother, who raised me from a small child, told me to wash my hands before dinner. Like most boys, I was not a big fan of washing my hands, and so I told her that Jesus said I didn't have to wash my hands before meals. Since my grandmother was a "Bible believing Christian" who believed in both the inerrancy and ultimate authority of the Bible, I figured I really had her this time. Instead, she gave me a lesson in humility and Biblical interpretation. "The Lord didn't say you shouldn't wash your hands before you sit down to table," she told me. "He just said that it isn't a sin not to. But in the same place, he said it *is* a sin not to honor your father and mother. So wash your hands and come to supper." And that's exactly what I did.

People who quote this passage to justify eating meat are like me quoting it to justify not washing my hands. They are twisting Jesus' words into a pretext for something that they want to do, instead of trying to understand and apply the real meaning.

Eat What Is Set before You

Luke 10:1–16 tells us that Jesus sent out seventy (according to some manuscripts, seventy-two) advance men to travel in pairs and visit the towns that he was planning to visit himself in the near future. In a pep talk before they set out, he told them to

> Carry no money belt, no bag, no shoes; and greet no one on the way. Whatever house you enter, first say, "Peace *be* to this house." . . . Stay in that house, eating and drinking what they give you; for the laborer is worthy of his wages. Do not keep moving from house to house. What-ever city you enter and they receive you, eat what is set before you; and heal those in it who are sick, and say to them, "The kingdom of God has come near to you." (Luke 10:4–9)

"Eat what is set before you," is widely interpreted to mean that the Seventy should eat meat if meat was what their hosts served them. But this is reading into the passage more than is there. In many ways Jesus' instructions are incomprehensible to us today, and it is probably wise not to try to parse them too closely. "Carry no money belt, no bag, no shoes; and greet no one on the road." The point is lost on us. But what does seem clear is that Jesus was not giving the Seventy dietary instructions. He was telling them how to behave when they arrived in a town. When Jesus told his emissaries to "eat what is set before you," he simply meant that they should be considerate house guests and not act like visiting big shots from out of town by insisting on fancy food or expensive delicacies. They would be living off the generosity of the family, probably a poor family, and they should share the simple, everyday fare of the household so as not to be a burden to their hosts.

In a few moments, we shall see that the early Jewish followers of Jesus, the Ebionites, were vegetarians. Since the Seventy would in all likelihood be staying in Ebionite homes, there was little or no chance that they would find meat set before them, and so the issue of flesh eating was not on Jesus' mind. He was talking about good manners as an expression of the humility that is proper for a servant of the gospel.

Locusts and Wild Honey

The New Testament portrays John the Baptist as the forerunner of Jesus, a man sent by God to proclaim his coming. According to the gospel of Mark, "John was clothed with camel's hair and *wore* a leather belt around his waist, and his diet was locusts and wild honey." (Mark 1:6; see also Matthew 3:4)

The Greek word for "locust" is *akris*, and that is the word used in both Mark and Matthew.[2] Some scholars have suggested that in this context *akris* does not mean "locust" at all, but refers

to the seed pod of the carob tree. This is possible because the
carob pod is edible, although not particularly appetizing; in the
ancient Middle East, it was eaten by the poor and used by the
rich to fatten livestock. Moreover, from ancient times the carob
pod has been known as "St. John's bread," and Christian legend
holds that it was John the Baptist's primary food. But Greek has
a different word for "carob pod," *keration*, which is used once in
the New Testament, in Luke 15:16.[3] *Akris*, on the other hand,
occurs twice more, and both times it unmistakably means
"locust" (Revelation 9:3,7).[4] That is what it appears to mean in
this instance, but this is by no means certain, and no matter
what *akris* means, it may be there by mistake.

The possibility of a copying error has been suggested by
several eminent scholars, including Richard Alan Young and
Keith Akers. In his *Panarion* ("Medicine Chest"), the fourth-
century theologian Epiphanius of Salamis provides the reme-
dies, in the form of orthodox responses, to no fewer than eighty
Christian heresies, including the teachings of Jewish Christians
known as Ebionites. He is upset because the Ebionite gospel
(now lost except for brief excerpts) describes John the Baptist's
diet not as locusts and honey, but as cakes dipped in honey, thus
contradicting the gospels.[5] The Greek word that Epiphanius
used to mean "cake" is *egkris*, which refers to something like a
pancake or a crepe, which it would be natural to eat with honey
just as we eat pancakes with syrup.[6] *Egkris* not only looks like
akris, it sounds like *akris*. If two copyists were working as a team,
one reading the text aloud while the other wrote the new copy
—which would be an efficient way to work—it would be easy for
the reader to say *egkris* and the writer to hear *akris*. Since locusts
are kosher,[7] and the Baptist had a reputation for eccentricity, the
substitution of *akris* for *egkris* would raise no eyebrows.

In any event, John the Baptist was not a vegan in the modern
sense, since he ate honey and wore a garment of camel's hair

cinched with a leather belt. But with the possible (and mystifying) exception of locusts, he did not eat the dead bodies of God's sentient creatures.

*   *   *

In history's first invocation of catch-22, Jesus remarked that "John the Baptist has come eating no bread and drinking no wine, and you say, 'He has a demon.' The Son of Man [Jesus] has come eating and drinking, and you say, 'Behold, a gluttonous man and a drunkard . . .' " (Luke 7:33–34) Matthew records the same comment, but omits the references to bread and wine, having Jesus say simply that "John came neither eating nor drinking." (Matthew 11:18–19) The NAB understands Luke's Greek word *artos*, "bread," figuratively and renders the phrase, "neither eating *food* nor drinking wine" (emphasis added). It is true that the New Testament sometimes uses "bread" to mean food generally, as in the Lord's Prayer, but that usage would be inappropriate here. Obviously, the Baptist ate "food," or he would have died of starvation instead of beheading. But more to the point, there is independent evidence that John the Baptist did, in fact, refuse to eat bread.

Our historical knowledge of the New Testament period comes largely from a Jewish aristocrat and adventurer turned historian named Flavius Josephus (37–*c*. 100). Composed in Greek (with the help of a Greek scribe) for a Roman audience, his massive *Antiquities of the Jews* and *The Jewish War* narrate the history of the people of Israel from the Garden of Eden to the conclusion of the disastrous revolt against Rome that erupted in 66 CE. *The Jewish War* was written first, and in it Josephus tells us that he had composed an earlier version in either Hebrew or Aramaic for the benefit of Jews living in Parthia, the successor to the old Babylonian and Persian Empires. These Parthian Jews were constantly encouraging Palestinian Jews to revolt, and Josephus—who had deserted to the Romans during the rebellion and now lived in luxury under the patronage of the Emperor—wanted to show them how futile and destructive this policy was.

In 1929 a New Testament scholar named Robert Eisler focused worldwide attention on a long-neglected manuscript written in Slavonic, a language that had been spoken in Russia during the middle ages and survives in the liturgy of the Russian Orthodox church. It appeared to be a version of *The Jewish War*, but with numerous variations and additional passages. Scholars had previously dismissed it as a corrupted version of the *War*, but Eisler argued that the "Slavonic Josephus" was actually a translation of Josephus' original Aramaic work, and therefore more truthful than the Greek *War*, which Josephus had slanted to flatter his Roman patrons. Scholars have lined up on both sides of the debate, and the issue has never been resolved.

In a remarkable passage, the Slavonic Josephus describes John the Baptist as "just like a bodiless spirit. His lips knew no bread; not even at the Passover did he taste unleavened bread . . . To wine and intoxicating drink he let himself not even draw near. And every animal he abhorred, and every wrong he rebuked, and tree-produce served him for use."[8] Because of the reference to Passover bread, there can be no doubt that here "bread" means bread, not "food." The phrase "every animal he abhorred," in conjunction with "tree-produce served him for use" clearly indicates a vegan diet and even points us back in the direction of carob pods.

But that raises another question. If John the Baptist did refuse to eat bread, as both Jesus and the Slavonic Josephus claim, we have to wonder whether "cakes" were considered a form of bread. If they were, John could not have eaten them, and must have eaten locusts—or carob pods—as our gospel manuscripts state. But the ancients may not have referred to them as "bread," any more than we would say "bread" when we meant "pancakes." "God," as the saying goes, "is in the details." And many of the details of the ancient world have been lost forever.

However that may be, Jesus' statement that "the Son of Man came eating and drinking" refers only to the bread and wine that John refused to indulge in. It cannot be used to support a claim that Jesus ate animal products.

Holy from His Birth

Eusebius Pamphilus (260–340 CE) was bishop of Caesaria in Judea, personal friend of the Emperor Constantine, and a key participant in the church councils that established Christian orthodoxy during the first half of the fourth century. Eusebius also composed a history of Christianity, commonly referred to as *Historia Ecclesiae*, "The History of the Church."

In his history, Eusebius tells of strict veganism in Jesus' immediate family. Quoting Hegesippus, a Christian writer from the early second century whose works are now lost except for brief excerpts quoted by later writers, Eusebius says that "Control of the Church passed to the apostles, together with the Lord's brother James, whom everyone from the Lord's time till our own has called the Righteous, for there were many Jameses, but this one was holy from his birth; he drank no wine or intoxicating liquor and ate no animal food; no razor came near his head; he did not smear himself with oil, and took no baths. He alone was permitted to enter the Holy Place [i.e., the "Holy of Holies," the most sacred precinct of the Temple in Jerusalem, which usually only the High Priest was allowed to enter] for his garments were not of wool but of linen."[9]

This particular James, often called "James the Just" or "James the Righteous"—who is not to be confused with the James who had been a commercial fisher—is mentioned several times in Acts (e.g., 12:17, 15:13–21), where he is clearly the leader of the

Christian Community. St. Paul speaks of him as such and like Hegesippus refers to him as "the Lord's brother" (Galatians 1:19). The Catholic Church recognizes James as the first bishop of Jerusalem. Protestants, Jews, and secular historians take the phrase "the Lord's brother" literally, considering him to be a younger son of Mary and Joseph. Catholics, who believe in the perpetual virginity of Mary, teach that James was either Joseph's son by a previous marriage, and therefore Jesus' step-brother, or his first cousin. Either way, here we have testimony reaching back to the very beginnings of Christianity that a member of Jesus' closest family was raised as a vegan.

It does not necessarily follow that since James was raised to be vegan, Jesus was, too. It seems likely, but there is always the chance that some special dedication or vow required James to be raised differently. What is certain is that in Jesus' family, veganism—even to the extent of not wearing wool clothing—was seen as a sign of righteousness and the epitome of ethical conduct.

Blessed Are the Poor

In addition to James the Just, ancient sources portray several of the Twelve Apostles as vegetarians. Perhaps most importantly, *The Clementine Recognitions*, a third-century work that reflects the traditions of the original Jewish Christians, the Ebionites, tells us that Peter lived primarily on bread supplemented with olives and, occasionally, vegetable soup.[10] During the nineteenth and most of the twentieth centuries, scholars universally rejected the *Recognitions* as a work of pious historical fiction, written to justify the doctrines of a small heretical sect. But the Dead Sea Scrolls are giving scholars an ever clearer picture of the religious environment in which Jesus lived and taught—and forcing students of the New Testament to rethink their casual dismissal of the *Recognitions*. Robert Eisenman, one of the leading Dead

Sea Scroll scholars in the world today, goes so far as to say that on many historical matters, the *Recognitions* may present a more accurate picture than Acts.[11] Keith Akers, an extremely rigorous scholar and historian of early Christianity, believes that *The Clementine Recognitions* and a related work entitled *The Clementine Homilies* represent the authentic recollections and teachings of the earliest Jewish Christians, the Ebionites, who had learned their practices directly from Jesus.[12] If Eisenman (who is not an advocate for vegetarianism or animal rights) and Akers (who is an advocate for both) are right about the Clementine literature—and they make an impressive case—the likelihood that Jesus was a vegetarian increases dramatically.

In his book *The Tutor*, St. Clement of Alexandria (died 215), one of the Greek fathers of the church, said that Matthew, one of the original Twelve Apostles, lived on "seeds, nuts, and vegetables, and no meat."[13] The *Acts of Thomas*, a third-century Christian work that describes the Apostle's travels to India, says that he "eats only bread with salt, and his drink is water . . ."[14] Rather than a given name, "Thomas" is actually a Hebrew nickname. It means "twin," and early Christian legend holds that Thomas was the twin brother of Jesus himself. And so we are tantalized by a second story of veganism in Jesus' immediate family and reminded that bread is the only food the gospels tell us that Jesus ate except for the single piece of fish.

We have already seen that the first Christians—the original Jewish followers of Jesus in Palestine—called themselves *ebionim*, or "Ebionites," which means "the poor." In the fourth century, the Ebionites were attacked as heretics by the Christian theologian and polemicist Epiphanius, whom we mentioned in connection with the Feeding of the Five Thousand. In his *Panarion*, Epiphanius tells us that the Ebionites were vegetarians who opposed animal sacrifice.[15] Unlike the later gentile Christians, who followed the teachings of St. Paul, the Ebionites learned their practices directly from Jesus, and so their lifestyle reflected his guidance and example.

Notes

1. We regard the heart, at least poetically, as the seat of the will and the emotions. But in the ancient world, the heart was believed to be the seat of the intellect. The stomach was considered the seat of the will and the emotions. (Picture a moonlit night, soft music, and the tender words, "I love you with all my stomach.") So when Jesus said "Wicked thoughts proceed from the heart," he meant that they proceed from the mind.
2. Strong number 200. See Thayer, p. 24; Vine, p. 375.
3. Strong number 2769. Wigram, *Greek Concordance,* p. 421.
4. Wigram, *Greek Concordance,* p. 26.
5. Epiphanius, *Panarion*, 30.13.4–5, in Barnestone, p. 337.
6. Young, p. 92; Akers, pp. 42–43.
7. Leviticus 11:22.
8. Quoted in Dunkerley, p. 43.
9. Eusebius, *History of the Church, 2.23.4.*
10. *Recognitions*, 7.6.
11. Eisenman, pp. 603–607.
12. Akers, 2000, pp. 24–26.
13. *Pedagogos*, 2.1.
14. *The Acts of Thomas*, in Barnstone, p. 471.
15. Akers, 2000, p. 27. See also Young, p. 97.

12: The Sparrow and the Lamb

I n the last two chapters, we have seen that—with the exception of fish—the Bible provides no evidence that Jesus or his disciples ate or drank animal products, not even lamb at the Last Supper. We have seen that the gospels portray John the Baptist—of whom Jesus said, "Among those born of women there has not arisen *anyone* greater than John the Baptist!" (Matthew 11:11)—as a strict vegetarian with the possible exception of locusts. We have seen that ancient Christian traditions depict two members of Jesus' immediate family as vegans: his brother (or step-brother or first cousin), James the Just, who was the first Christian bishop of Jerusalem; and the man alleged to be Jesus' twin brother, St. Thomas the Apostle. These same traditions describe two more of the Twelve Apostles—Simon Peter and Matthew—as vegans. And finally, we have seen that the earliest followers of Jesus, the Jewish Christians known as Ebionites, who learned their practices directly from Jesus, were vegetarian. By any reasonable standard of historical evidence, the claim that Jesus was a vegan has to be taken seriously.

As to fish, the situation is more muddled. We saw the gospels connect Jesus with fish, fishing, or fishers on seven occasions: once when he called four commercial fishers to quit their trade and become his disciples; twice when he miraculously multiplied a few cooked fish belonging to someone else and distributed them to a crowd; once when he told Simon Peter to go fishing for a fish who held a coin in his mouth; once when he asked what father would give his son a scorpion if the child asked for a fish; once, after the resurrection, when he is said to have eaten a morsel of fish to prove to his disciples that he was not a ghost; and once, also after the resurrection, when he is described as cooking fish by the Sea of Galilee and offering them to his disciples for breakfast. None of this rises to the level of proof, and it certainly does not suggest that fish was a staple of Jesus' diet, but this frequent mention of fish and fishing forces us to wonder.

Overall, the evidence concerning Jesus' diet (except for bread) is meager and largely circumstantial, while the arguments on both sides of the question are speculative. None is conclusive one way or the other. If I were a Las Vegas bookmaker, I would give you ten to one that—apart from fish—Jesus never ate or drank animal products and followed the vegan diet prescribed in Genesis 1:29. But my odds that Jesus never ate fish would be more like even money.

That's where I come out. But other students of Christian origins look at the same evidence and come away with conclusions that stand a good ways off from mine—some to the right, others to the left. Andrew Linzey, Christianity's best known animal rights theologian, concludes that "Jesus certainly ate fish and possibly meat. . ."[1] while theology professor Richard Alan Young believes that "There doesn't seem to be any good reason to reject the Biblical traditions about Jesus eating fish."[2] On the opposite side are scholars like Rynn Berry, who says that "Although the evidence for Jesus' vegetarianism is largely circumstantial, it is nonetheless compelling."[3] Keith Akers puts it more bluntly: ". . . Jesus taught and practiced vegetarianism. . ."[4]

The fact that meticulous scholars who are ethical vegetarians can study the evidence and come to opposite conclusions underscores that we cannot determine with any degree of historical confidence whether or not Jesus was a vegetarian. The only way we could model our diet after Jesus' would be to eat nothing but bread, since bread is all we know for certain that he ate.

Mad Pig Disease

The gospels record only three instances in which Jesus is said to have had direct contact with animals. In the cleansing of the Temple, which we discussed above, he liberated animals about to be sacrificed. In the affair of the Gadarene pigs, which we will consider in a moment, he is said to have allowed demons to enter the bodies of pigs, who were driven insane and drowned themselves in the Sea of Galilee. Finally, several days before his crucifixion, in an event known as the Triumphal Entry into Jerusalem—which Christians commemorate on Palm Sunday—Jesus briefly rode on a donkey to fulfill a prophecy in the Hebrew scriptures that the messiah would appear riding on a donkey.[5] Except for this one event, which was brief and carefully staged, the gospels invariably describe Jesus as travelling on foot, even when he was going from Galilee to Jerusalem, a journey of nearly a hundred miles.

* * *

The affair of the Gadarene pigs began when Jesus encountered a man who was possessed by demons. The demons begged Jesus not to drive them out with no place to go, but to send them into a herd of two thousand pigs who were eating nearby. When Jesus agreed, the demons left the man and entered the pigs, who promptly dashed headlong into the Sea of Galilee and drowned. (Matthew 8:28–34, Mark 5:1–20, Luke 8:26–39)

Defenders of vivisection sometimes remind us that this story shows Jesus killing two thousand animals for the health of one human being. Although animal rights advocates sometimes quibble about whether Jesus "sent" the demons into the pigs or merely "allowed" them to enter the pigs, the thrust of the story does seem to be as the vivisectors describe it. Still, there are problems.

First, the text demonstrates that the story existed in several versions and underwent changes over time, after the fashion of folk legends. Mark and Luke tell us that the demons possessed one man; Matthew says two. Different ancient manuscripts give different locations. Some say the territory of the "Gadarenes," some say "Gerasenes," and others "Gergesenes." Gadara was a town about five miles southeast of the Sea of Galilee, while Gerasa was about thirty miles southeast of Gadara. The location of Gergesa is uncertain, but scholars believe that it may have been at the site of present-day Khersa, on the eastern shore of the Sea of Galilee. Gadara and Gerasa were part of a territory called the Decapolis, the Ten Cities, which was a confederation of Greek city-states with almost no Jewish population. This would at least explain the presence of a large herd of pigs (which Jews would not raise because they were "unclean" animals), but it creates another problem because both were too far from the Sea of Galilee for the pigs to drown themselves in it. The proposed site for Gergesa is on the shore of the Sea of Galilee, but it is in a territory that in Jesus' day was officially called Gaulanitis, in an area that was popularly thought of as part of Galilee, where the population was almost exclusively Jewish, which makes the presence of the pigs difficult to explain.

Secondly, even today two thousand pigs is a large herd for a free-range farm. In the first century, it would have been huge. The owner of a herd of that size would have been a man of great wealth and influence, and Jesus' action would have cost him a sizable fortune. More importantly, the drowning of the pigs would have been taken as a political act of aggression, a Jewish nationalist protest against Roman rule over the land of Israel. The "unclean" pigs would have been seen as effigies of the "unclean" gentiles who ruled Israel, and their drowning would have been interpreted as a call for patriotic Jews to drive their gentile masters "into the sea," i.e., the Mediterranean, and back to Rome where they belonged. There had been a bloody anti-Roman rebellion two decades earlier, in 7 CE, and there would be another in 66. During Jesus' ministry, rebel guerrilla bands were active throughout the country, and Luke mentions an "insurrection" in Jerusalem that involved "murder," and speaks of "the Galileans whose blood Pilate had mixed with their sacrifices," presumably because they had tried to seize the Temple by force during the uprising.[6] Israel was a tinderbox.

It seems incredible that Jesus could send two thousand pigs to their deaths in the Sea of Galilee without setting off a legal and political firestorm, especially since all three gospels tell us that the swineherds spread the story far and wide. But we never hear of repercussions. In the politically superheated atmosphere of Roman-occupied Israel, we would expect Jesus to be arrested, interrogated, punished, and forced to either make restitution to the owner of the pigs or become the man's slave. That is how things were done in the Roman Empire, where the principal sources of slaves were prisoners of war, orphans, and debtors. And when we recall that Jesus was a Jew who had destroyed the property of a member of the gentile ruling class, that is even more what we would expect. But nothing of the kind transpires. Jesus goes on his way undisturbed. No one seems to care. It is as if nothing had happened.

And that, I believe, is the real state of affairs. Nothing did happen. The story of the Gadarene pigs is a legend that originated in anti-Roman nationalism and attached itself to Jesus.

Some will argue that whether the story is factually true does not matter; the important point is that its inclusion in the gospels demonstrates that early Christians approved of killing animals for human benefit. Obviously, it shows that *some* early Christians—those who edited the gospels—approved of killing animals for human benefit. But they were gentiles, as we can see from their failure to appreciate the political subtext of the story and their confusion over where the drowning of the pigs took place. From the days of Saint Paul, whom we shall discuss shortly, many gentile Christians have held animals in low regard. No one disputes that tragic fact, which over the centuries has been responsible for so much suffering and death. But this attitude originated with Paul and cannot be traced back beyond him. It has no connection to Jesus and his immediate followers, and the legend of the Gadarene pigs does nothing to establish one.

Scraps for the Dogs and a Little Lost Lamb

The gospels record four occasions on which Jesus spoke of animals in a way that could give us insight into how he regarded them. They are a mixed bag.

To begin with the negative, Matthew and Mark tell of a gentile woman who asked Jesus to cure her daughter of mental illness. Jesus refused, saying "It is not proper to take the children's bread and throw it to the dogs." The woman agreed, but pointed out that even "the dogs feed on the crumbs which fall from their masters' table." Impressed by her humility and faith, Jesus relented and healed her daughter. (Matthew 15:22–28; see Mark 7:25–30)

We have already noted that Jesus is here portrayed as a bigot who holds gentiles in contempt. This story also suggests that he shared the low opinion of dogs that has been common in the Middle East from antiquity to the present. Both of those views are contained in the one statement; they cannot be disentangled. Anyone who holds dogs (or animals in general) in low regard because of this statement would also have to hold gentiles in low regard. Christians who are not willing to do the latter have no basis on which to do the former.

Beyond that, the fact that Jesus appears to have held a low opinion of dogs does not mean that he would approve of exploiting or abusing them. I know many dedicated animal rights advocates, for example, who find spiders or snakes repulsive, but who still refuse to harm them. In the absence of further evidence, we simply do not know.

Jesus mentioned dogs on another occasion as well. In the Sermon on the Mount, Matthew quotes him as saying, "Do not give what is holy to dogs, and do not throw your pearls before swine, or they will trample them under their feet, and turn and tear you to pieces." (Matthew 7:6) We have just heard Jesus call gentiles "dogs," and seen that to ancient Jews pigs were "unclean" animals, just as gentiles were "unclean" human beings, sinners by definition. And so it seems likely that Jesus was using "dogs" and "pigs" as stand-ins for "gentiles." He was saying here what he had said to the woman whose daughter was ill: Gentiles are not fit to receive the gospel, any more than dogs and pigs are fit to receive fine jewels. Again, anyone who believes that this statement justifies human exploitation of animals would also have to believe that only Jews can be Christians and gentiles should not be preached the gospel. The two concepts are inextricably intertwined.

But that is not the only way this statement can reasonably be read. When we say, "Don't take a bull into a china shop," we don't necessarily mean any disrespect to the bull. Bulls are perfectly fine in open pastures, but they are not designed to navigate narrow aisles lined with delicate china; and being unable to appreciate the value of items that to them are useless, they make no effort to try. Our modern saying simply means that people should not be placed in situations they are not equipped to handle. In the language of his day, Jesus may have been making much the same point, saying that the gospel should be taught only to those who were mentally and spiritually prepared to receive it. Either interpretation is possible, and there is no way to be certain which is correct.

* * *

Jesus' most famous comment on the relative value of animals and humans is found in Matthew and also in Luke. "Are not two sparrows sold for a cent? And *yet* not one of them will fall to the ground apart from your Father . . . So do not fear, you are more valuable than many sparrows." (Matthew 10:29–31; see Luke 12:6–7. A variation is found in Matthew 6:26.) This saying is frequently quoted on both sides of the animal rights debate. Supporters claim that it shows that animals are important to God in their own right and we have an obligation as God's stewards not to exploit them for our own purposes. Opponents see it as proof that God values animals less than human beings, and we may, therefore, exploit them as we please.

Guidance on how we should interpret Jesus' remark about sparrows comes in the form of a parable that is also found in both Matthew and Luke. "If any man has a hundred sheep, and one of them has gone astray, does he not leave the ninety-nine on the mountains and go and search for the one that is straying? If it turns out that he finds it, truly I say to you, he rejoices over it more than over the ninety-nine which have not gone astray." (Matthew 18:12–13; see Luke 15:3–6) Ninety-nine sheep represented a considerable economic investment. By comparison, the value of one sheep was negligible. Yet Jesus approved of the shepherd leaving the ninety-nine untended to rescue the one from fear, hunger, and likely injury or death. And so, the first lesson we can take away from this story is that the interests of the "less valuable" should not be sacrificed to the interests of the "more valuable." *Each individual has an irreducible core of inherent worth that make the question of "greater or lesser value" irrelevant to issues of ethical consideration.* Thus when Jesus said that humans were worth more than sparrows, he was not saying that a sparrow's well-being could be sacrificed for human purposes, but only that God's concern for the sparrow is assurance that we can count on God to take good care of us.

The second lesson in this parable is that *our dominion ought to be exercised more for the well-being of individual animals than for the welfare of populations or species.* Jesus did not view the one hundred sheep as a "flock," or any kind of collective; he viewed them as one hundred individuals, each of whom was important in his or her own right. This is a direct refutation of conservationists and environmentalists who work to sustain "healthy populations" and save species from extinction while at the same time promoting activities like hunting, fishing, and trapping that inflict suffering and death on individual animals. There can be no question that protecting the environment is a vital undertaking. But, according to Jesus, an environmentalism that preserves species and ecosystems while ignoring the suffering of individual animals is morally deficient.

Pigs in a Blanket

Acts tells us that forty days following his resurrection, Jesus ascended into heaven.[7] Sometime after this, a Roman army officer named Cornelius, who was stationed in Caesaria Maritima ("Caesar's City by the Sea"), the administrative capital of Roman Judea, received a vision from God telling him to get in touch with Simon Peter, who was staying in Caesaria at the time. Simultaneously, Peter, who was unaware of Cornelius, also received a vision, in which he saw animals—both kosher and unkosher—being lowered from heaven in a blanket, while a heavenly voice told him to kill them and eat them. Peter refused, saying that he had never eaten anything that was impure. The heavenly voice then told him not to judge impure what God had purified. When he came out of his trance, "Peter was greatly perplexed in mind as to what the vision which he had seen might be." While he was trying to unravel it, messengers from Cornelius arrived with the story of their master's vision. Now Peter understood. "You yourselves know how unlawful it is for a man who is a Jew to associate with a foreigner or to visit him; and *yet* God has shown me that I should not call any man unholy or unclean." (Acts 10:28)

Christians who defend meat eating often claim that God was telling Saint Peter in this vision that he should have no qualms about eating meat, including meat that was not kosher. But Peter's vision had nothing to do with animals or eating meat. It was a symbolic message that gentiles (represented by the unkosher animals) as well as Jews (represented by the kosher animals) should be accepted into the Christian community. That is how Peter himself understood it, and that is how the author of Acts understood it as well.

The Imitation of Christ

I have devoted so much space to the question of whether Jesus was a vegetarian because Christian meat eaters often defend their diet by citing the New Testament doctrine that Jesus was morally perfect and without sin.[8] Since the gospels tell us that Jesus cooked, distributed, and ate fish, so this argument runs, we can eat meat with a clear conscience.

Although many Christians consider this an irrefutable argument, it was, in fact, refuted by Jesus himself, who emphatically denied that he was without sin. Mark 10:17–18 tells us that a man ran up to Jesus "and knelt before Him, and asked Him, 'Good Teacher, what shall I do to inherit eternal life?' And Jesus said to him, 'Why do you call Me good? No one is good except God alone.' "[9]

But aside from that, the bottom line is that we do not know enough about the circumstances and details of Jesus' life to base our own lives on it, except in broad outline. And that outline is as clear and eloquent as the details are garbled and obscure. Jesus identified with the poor, the powerless, and the oppressed, and he devoted his life their service. If we would model our lives after his, we must do the same, and in our modern world, there are none poorer, more powerless, and more oppressed than the animals.

The phrase "lamb of God" refers to the lambs that were ritually slaughtered and eaten every Passover. When the New Testament calls Jesus "the lamb of God,"[10] it identifies him with the victims of sacrifice rather than its perpetrators, that is to say, with the animals who suffer at the hands of humanity, not with those who inflict the suffering. Jesus accepted this identification at the Last Supper, which is portrayed in three of the gospels as a Passover meal, when he said of the bread which took the place of the lamb, "Take, eat; this is My body." (Matthew 26:26) By identifying his own execution with the killing of animals by human beings, Jesus was saying that, "Just as my death is unjust, so is theirs." This identification with all who suffer, which includes the poor, the oppressed, and the animals, forms the ethical text of Jesus' life and death. That is the example that those who would practice the imitation of Christ are called to follow, not the tiny—and ultimately indecipherable—footnote that says he may have eaten fish.

This is where our extended look at Jesus' diet has brought us. The footnote really is indecipherable. Because it is suggestive without being conclusive, we cannot read it either way with confidence. Therefore, the question that matters is not the unanswerable, Did Jesus eat fish? It is rather, If we would truly live in the spirit of Jesus' life and teaching, how will we treat God's sentient living souls?

Notes

1. Linzey, 1991, p. 47.
2. Young, p. 3.
3. Berry, 1999, p. 53.
4. Akers, 1989, p. 174.
5. Matthew 21:1–11, Mark 11:1–10, Luke 19:29–44, John 12:12–19. The prophecy is found in Zechariah 9:9.
6. Luke 13:1 and 23:19.
7. Acts 1:3, 9.
8. See, for example, 2 Corinthians 5:21, Hebrews 4:15, 1 Peter 2:21–22, and 1 John 3:5.
9. This incident is also reported in Matthew 19:16–17 and Luke 18:18–19.
10. John 1:29, 36.

13: The Gospel of Mercy

The earliest books of the Hebrew Scriptures report some of the first known interjections of authentic inspiration into a dialogue heretofore dominated by human nature and cultural tradition. This inspiration, with its call for boundless love and compassion, was taken up by the Later Prophets, who condemned the excesses of the rich and powerful and demanded justice for the weak and oppressed. In fearless and eloquent language they decried the plight of widows, orphans, and sacrificial animals—in fact, all who suffered at the hands of the mighty—and implored us to live solely by the law of love.

This was the call that Jesus took up when he began his ministry. He declared "You shall love your neighbor as yourself" to be one of the two Prime Directives of the human race. He told us to do unto others as we would have others do unto us. And with the prophets, he excoriated the wealthy "who devour widows' houses" (Mark 12:38–40) and condemned the sacrifice of animals, whom he called "the innocent." (Matthew 12:7)

The Last Shall Be First

Earlier, we talked about the Hierarchy of Service, in which the powerful and privileged have a moral obligation to nurture and protect the weak and vulnerable. *Jesus made the Hierarchy of Service the theme of his gospel.* "If anyone wants to be first," he said, "he shall be last of all and servant of all." (Mark 9:35) Even more explicitly, Jesus told his disciples, "You know that those who are recognized as rulers of the Gentiles lord it over them; and their great men exercise authority over them. But it is not this way among you, but whoever wishes to become great among you shall be your servant; and whoever wishes to be first among you shall be slave of all. For even the Son of Man [i.e., Jesus himself] did not come to be served but to serve, and to give His life a ransom for many." (Mark 10:42–45)

In the world of Greek philosophy, moral obligations flowed up the hierarchy; the lower owed service to the higher. In the gospel of Jesus, it is just the opposite; the higher owe service to the lower. Viewed another way, the Hierarchy of Service is the hierarchy of privilege turned upside down. As the French say, *Noblesse oblige*. "Nobility obligates," it does not entitle. A hierarchy based on entitlement is arrogance institutionalized; it is an alibi for rapaciousness. A hierarchy based on service is the Prime Directives put into practice; it is the dominion of love. We love God by serving God's creation. We love our neighbors by serving our neighbors, and the farther they stand below us in the hierarchy of power—the more they stand in need of our help—the greater is our moral obligation to serve them. Humankind stands at the top of the hierarchy of power. Our nonhuman neighbors stand at the bottom. Our moral obligation to serve them is absolute.

Blessed Are the Merciful

In the opening section of the Sermon on the Mount, known as the "Beatitudes," Jesus listed nine characteristics that can lead to happiness in the Kingdom of Heaven. (Matthew 5:3–12) Several, like "mourning" and "being persecuted" are misfortunes that come unbidden. They are included to comfort the afflicted and teach compassion. But others are qualities that we exhibit when we follow the Prime Directives. They form a training manual for exercising the dominion of love. I will quote them in the familiar King James Version.

Blessed are the meek: for they shall inherit the earth.
Meekness is the quality that causes us never to seek our own advantage through the suffering of another. The opposite of meekness is arrogance, and just as arrogance arises out of pride and selfishness, meekness is the child of love and compassion. As such, it is the quality that most clearly displays the image of God in our lives. It is arrogance, not meekness, to expropriate and consume the treasures of the earth for our own benefit. I like to think of this as the Environmental Beatitude, because it reminds us that if we practice meekness, the Earth will nurture us for countless generations, but if we practice arrogance, our children will inherit a desert created by our own rapacious consumption. Sometimes, in the words of the old saying, we are not punished *for* our sins, we are punished *by* our sins.

But "Blessed are the meek" is not just the Environmental Beatitude. To claim that our appetites, pleasure, and convenience are more important than the lives of animals is also arrogance, and not meekness. God gives no greater gift than life; it is precious to all who receive it. To steal God's gift from those who have been placed in our care simply because we like the taste of their flesh or hope to buy our own health at the price of their sickness and death mocks Jesus' gospel.

Blessed are they which do hunger and thirst after righteousness: for they shall be filled.
The cheeseburger may taste good, but it leaves us hungry for something that we can't quite identify. And so we try to silence our hunger by eating bigger and better cheeseburgers, but to no avail, because the hunger we feel is not for beef and cheese, but

righteousness, and what is disturbing our peace of mind is a conscience that knows we are practicing cruelty, not love, when we eat the flesh of living souls. The soy burger tastes just as good, but it leaves no bitter spiritual aftertaste, because we know that our meal brought no suffering and death to helpless creatures who had done us no harm. It fills the soul as well as the stomach.

Blessed are the merciful: for they shall obtain mercy.
The more deeply someone can be damaged by our cruelty, the greater is our obligation to show mercy. And our cruelty damages no one more deeply than the defenseless animals on whom we turn our terrible power. To deny our mercy to those who need it most is to deny the gospel of Christ. As Reverend Primatt told us, "Cruelty is atheism." If "Blessed are the meek" is the Environmental Beatitude, "Blessed are the merciful" is the Animal Rights Beatitude.

Blessed are the pure in heart: for they shall see God.
This Beatitude urges us to be alert to the insidious quality that permits us to withhold our mercy from those who need it most: self-deception in the service of our own pleasures. When we are pure in heart, our motives are pure; we have no hidden agendas; we do not do something for one reason and tell ourselves that we are doing it for another. When we are pure in heart, we do not pretend that our arrogance is God's grace, that our rapaciousness is God's bounty, or that we are cruel with God's blessing. If we are pure in heart, we use the God-given intelligence of which we are so proud to find ways to help the helpless; we do not use it to think up clever and sophisticated rationalizations for exploiting and abusing them.

We eat meat, eggs, and cheese and drink milk because we like their taste; we wear leather shoes and fur coats because we enjoy their look and feel; we hunt and fish because we enjoy killing; we go to circuses and zoos because we value our pleasure over the animals' suffering; and we experiment on animals because we hope to protect ourselves from pain, debility, and despair that are usually less severe than what we inflict upon them. When we are pure in heart, these motives are not hidden behind a screen of alibis and sophistry. We do not construct subtle philosophical and theological arguments to justify our appetites. We do not tell ourselves, in the face of common sense and scientific evidence, that animals cannot really suffer, at least not the way we do, or that they are not "self-aware" and therefore don't know that they're suffering. We do not tell ourselves that God placed these sensitive, life-affirming creatures here as resources for us, and that their suffering doesn't matter because it's God's will. We do not tell ourselves that the "food chain" is a "law of nature," and since we are at the top of it we have a right to kill and eat everyone else on the planet. If we are pure in heart, we can give ourselves an honest look and recognize our motives for what they are. And once we do that, the sophistries and rationalizations become as insubstantial as the emperor's new clothes in the fairy tale. They can no longer conceal the evil that we are doing, and once we recognize the evil, most of us can no longer keep doing it. It is far easier to do evil in the name of good than in its own name. Slavery was practiced in the name of good. Segregation was practiced in the name of good. The Nazi death camps and Soviet gulags were created in the name of good. And the eternal Treblinka operates in the name of good.

These lies that we tell ourselves not only hide the evil that we do; they also hide God from our sight—or, more precisely, they block us from the presence of God. God is always open to us; it is we who are unable to experience God because of the impurity of our hearts. When we are pure in heart, we see God, and we know that "God is the Compassionate One," "God is love," and God's love and compassion extend to every living soul in the universe. And we know that if we are to live in the image of God, our love and compassion must likewise extend to all the living souls who find themselves in our dominion.

Blessed are the peacemakers: for they shall be called the children of God. Our relationship with animals is a relationship of violence. We deny them the right to live according to their natures, the way God created them to live; we force them to live—and die— according to our desires. We destroy their homes and their habitat, we imprison them, beat them, kill them, do whatever it takes to turn them into instruments of our pleasure. With the animals, we are not peacemakers; we are not even warriors— which connotes some degree of fairness, equality, and honor— we are despots, tyrants, and dictators. We savage noncombatant populations with hardly a second thought. As Isaac Bashevis Singer told us, we force the animals to live under a totalitarian regime that equals in cruelty Hitler's Third Reich and Stalin's Soviet Union. A life based on violence toward animals is a violent life, no matter how peacefully we may live in other respects. It is not a fitting life for anyone who aspires to live as a child of God.

14: Does God Care about Oxen?

When Christians want to defend human exploitation of animals, the New Testament figure they turn to most often is Saint Paul, and with some reason, for Paul flatly discounts the Hebrew Scriptures' teaching about animals. Earlier, we saw that Deuteronomy 25:4, "You shall not muzzle the ox while he is threshing," forms the basis of the Jewish doctrine of *tsar ba'ale chayim*, which makes it a religious duty for Jews to treat animals with kindness and concern for their physical and emotional well-being. In 1 Corinthians 9:9–14, Paul quotes this verse and asks, "God is not concerned about oxen, is He? Or is He speaking altogether for our sake? Yes, for our sake it was written." He then proceeds to explain this verse as an allegory instructing that preachers ought to be paid for their services.[1]

Faced with the ineluctable fact that the Hebrew Scriptures clearly portray God as concerned about oxen and other animals, some commentators have denied that Paul actually said what he appears to have said. John Wesley, for example, says that God's commandments that we show mercy to animals are "by no means contradicted by St. Paul's question: 'Doth God take care for oxen?' Without doubt, he does. We cannot deny it without flatly denying his word. The plain meaning of the Apostle is, Is this all that is implied in the text? Hath it not a farther meaning?

Does it not teach us, we are to feed the bodies of those whom we desire to feed our souls?"[2]

Wesley's claim has some plausibility, because the Greek word that the NASB translates "altogether" in Paul's question "Or is he speaking altogether for our sake?" is *pantos,* which has two distinct meanings. The first is "wholly," "entirely," "in every way," which is how the translators of the NASB read it. The second meaning of *pantos* is "certainly," "definitely," "undoubtedly," which is how the translators of the NIV read it when they translate this sentence, "Surely, he says this for us, doesn't he?"[3]

But even if we give Paul the benefit of the doubt and accept the view of Wesley and the NIV translators that *pantos* was merely intended to add emphasis to Paul's point, and not to restrict Deuteronomy 25:4 to one interpretation, there are no actual words in this passage that support Wesley's understanding of Paul's question. Paul does not say, "God isn't *only* concerned about oxen, is he? Didn't he *also* say this for us? It was written for us *as well.*" As much as I would like to find Wesley's meaning in Paul's words, I cannot. I think Wesley was able to find it only because he could not bring himself to accept that Paul would so blatantly contradict the plain message of the Hebrew Scriptures and Jesus. But Paul did contradict them, and the key to understanding why lies in his unusual background and the Herculean task that he set for himself.

A Jew, a Greek, and a Roman

His Hebrew name was *Shaul,* but Greek has no "sh" sound and no letter to represent it, so in the New Testament he became *Saulos.* In English, we drop the Greek ending and call him "Saul." After becoming a Christian, he stopped using his Hebrew name altogether and was known only by his Latin name, *Paulus,* or Paul. According to Acts, he was born in Tarsus, a Greek city on the southern coast of modern-day Turkey.[4] In a speech, he claimed to have been raised and educated in Jerusalem,[5] but for someone educated in a city in which everyone—except for a wealthy and powerful elite—was intensely hostile to Greek civilization, Paul writes remarkably fluid Greek and displays an impressive knowledge of Greek culture. On the other hand, when he first appears on the scene, apparently still a young man, he is already in Jerusalem and an associate of the High Priest.[6] Another mystifying aspect of Paul's background is that he was a Roman citizen by birth, a privilege granted to very few Jews, usually men who had performed some important service for the Roman Empire and their descendants.[7]

The theory that most readily explains a Jerusalem education, fluent Greek, entrée to the highest circles of Jewish power, and Roman citizenship is that Paul was born into the small Jewish aristocracy who ran the Temple and collaborated with the Romans, helping to govern Israel on their behalf. We have to consider that Paul may even have been a member of the wealthiest and most powerful Jewish family in the Roman Empire, the Herods, since in one of his letters, he sends greetings to "Herodion [Little Herod or Herod, Jr.] my *kinsman.*" (Romans 16:11, emphasis added) Paul's Greek word is *syngenes*, which has the basic meaning of "relative" or "family member,"[8] but in Romans 9:3, he uses it figuratively to refer to Jews as his "kinsmen according to the flesh," and we cannot be absolutely certain that he is not using it the same way here, to mean "my fellow Jew." But even if he is, he is clearly on friendly terms with the Herod family, which suggests that he was a member of their class. In another letter, written from Rome, Paul sends along greetings from the Christians in "Caesar's household," suggesting that he was a friend of the Imperial family, as were the Herods. (Philippians 4:22)[9]

Originally, the family of the Herods, who ruled Palestine as puppets of the Romans on and off for nearly a century, were not Jews at all, but Idumeans, an Arab people who had been forcibly

converted to Judaism during the second century BCE by the
Jewish ruler John Hyrcanus. Around the middle of the following
century, an Idumean sheik and adventurer named Antipater
ingratiated himself with the Romans and became the most
powerful Jew in Judea. Antipater was assassinated by religious
nationalists who opposed Roman rule, but Augustus Caesar
appointed his son Herod king of Judea, and from 37 BCE until the
great rebellion in 66 CE, the Herodians were a force to be reck-
oned with in the Roman Empire. Friends of the imperial family,
rulers of both Jewish and gentile provinces, they were wealthy
sophisticates who boasted Greek as well as Jewish educations
and were more at home at Caesar's court than in the courtyards
of the Temple in Jerusalem. In fact, the Herodians seem never to
have adapted well to the restrictions of the Jewish law, and they
spent as much time as possible in gentile cities, where they could
enjoy a more liberal lifestyle. At least two generations of Herod
children were raised in the imperial compound in Rome, where
they were educated with the children of the imperial family. It is
small wonder that two hundred years after John Hyrcanus forced
the Idumeans to convert under threat of death, most Jews still
regarded the Herodians as insincere converts who kept up a
façade of Judaism to promote their political ambitions.

Because the emperors trusted them to govern the rebellious
Jewish provinces, the Herodians were one of the few families in
the Roman Empire who found it politically and financially
advantageous to be Jewish. If Paul was in fact, as seems likely, a
member of the family Herod, this would explain his support for
slavery and his belief that no reigning government should ever
be resisted, two of his more perplexing teachings that we
discussed earlier.

*   *   *

Paul first appears in Acts, sometime after the crucifixion of Jesus, as an agent of the High Priest whose job is to investigate and prosecute the followers of Jesus.[10] On the way to Damascus armed with arrest warrants for Christians, he experienced a vision of the resurrected Christ that transformed him from a persecutor of Christianity into one of its most zealous advocates.[11] As a member of an elite cosmopolitan Jewish family who could move easily among gentiles and Greek-speaking Jews overseas, Paul was a natural to spread the Christian message outside of Palestine. He had grown up straddling the spiritual world of Judaism and the social and political world of the Roman upper classes. His first effort to reconcile them had been to join himself to the priestly aristocracy who controlled the Temple in Jerusalem and who supported both the Romans and their allies, the Herodians. He became their agent in the campaign to root out the followers of a religious and social movement that challenged the legitimacy of the Temple cult. His second was to become a leader of that movement. The timing could not have been better.

The Apostle to the Gentiles

Paul came of age in a Roman Empire that was undergoing a spiritual upheaval. Exotic Eastern religions, such as Zoroastrianism, Mithraism, and the worship of the Egyptian goddess Isis, were all the rage. Judaism, which to the Romans was an exotic Eastern religion, enjoyed wide popularity among people attracted to its monotheism and strict ethical teachings. These people, drawn from all classes of society, were known as "friends" or "God-fearers." They studied the Hebrew Scriptures, attended synagogue, worshipped the Jewish God, and adhered to Jewish ethical standards. All around the eastern Mediterranean and as far west as Rome, they were a receptive audience for Paul, who was soon proclaiming himself the apostle to the gentiles.[12] But almost from the beginning, he ran head-on into a seemingly insurmountable problem.

The God-fearers wanted to worship the Jewish God, but they did not want to become part of the people of Israel. To put it another way, they wanted to become Judaists, but not Jews. And this was impossible. From time immemorial and down to the present, you cannot convert to Judaism without joining the Jewish people. Conversion to Judaism is adoption into the family of Abraham.

There were several reasons why gentiles attracted to Judaism were reluctant to convert and become Jews. First, anti-Semitism was rife in the Roman Empire. Jews were disliked, discriminated against, and rarely allowed to become Roman citizens. Becoming a Jew in the Roman Empire meant condemning yourself to a life without security or privileges. If by skill and hard work you managed to climb up the social ladder a ways, you never knew when you were going to be kicked back down to the bottom and lose everything you had worked for. Exacerbating this situation, Judea and Galilee had a well-deserved reputation as the most restless and rebellious provinces in the Empire. Almost from the time Pompey the Great captured Jerusalem in 63 BCE, they had launched one bloody uprising after another, and when there was no full-scale rebellion in progress, there was a continual low-grade guerrilla war being conducted by paramilitary units such as the dreaded Zealots. By definition, to be a Jew in the Roman Empire was to be suspected of being a traitor, and the gentile God-fearers had no wish to be tagged as traitors.

Second, men converting to Judaism had to be circumcised, and in the first century, adult circumcision was a painful and dangerous procedure with a high risk of infection. Furthermore, circumcision was not practiced by the Greeks and Romans, who regarded it as a barbaric form of ritual mutilation that no civilized person would consider. In an era of public baths and naked athletic competitions, few gentile men were willing to take on the humiliation of circumcision.

Finally, most gentiles, including those attracted to Judaism, found Jewish dietary laws pointless and burdensome. Among the wealthy, shellfish and pork were popular dishes, and among the middle class and the poor, they were delicacies that few wanted to forego on those rare occasions when they had the opportunity to indulge. And so the God-fearers hung around on the fringes of Judaism, but never made the leap. Nor would they make the leap to Christianity so long as becoming a Christian meant becoming a Jew, being circumcised, and taking on all of the Jewish law, including the kosher restrictions.

Drawing on his aristocratic, Judeo-Roman background, the apostle to the gentiles solved his seemingly insoluble problem by a gambit that is astonishing in its simplicity and daring. He proclaimed that there was now a way for gentiles to worship the Jewish god and follow Jewish ethical principles without having to keep kosher, be circumcised, or join the Jewish nation. By becoming Christians, gentiles could fulfill their dream of becoming Judaists without becoming Jews. The reason for this, he explained, was that the death and resurrection of Christ had rendered the Jewish law obsolete. The Covenant with Abraham and Moses had been replaced by a New Covenant that required only faith in Jesus Christ as the son of God who had been sacrificed for our sins and resurrected from the dead.[13] The fear of being suspected of treason he overcame by teaching that all governments, no matter how rapacious, including the Roman Empire, were ordained by God, making it a religious duty to submit to them in every respect. All the things that gentiles found objectionable in Judaism had been wiped out at a single stroke.

*   *   *

Paul had never met Jesus or heard him teach, nor did he learn his dramatic new message from any of Jesus' followers. It came to him, he announced, directly in a vision of the resurrected Christ. Paul was adamant on this point, because he considered this vision the basis of his authority to preach these new doctrines. He told the Christians in Galatia that

> the gospel which was preached by me is not according to man. For I neither received it from man, nor was I taught it, but *I received it* through a revelation of Jesus Christ . . . But when God, who had set me apart *even* from my mother's womb and called me through His grace, was pleased to reveal His Son in me so that I might preach Him among the Gentiles, I did not immediately consult with flesh and blood, nor did I go up to Jerusalem to those who were apostles before me; but I went away to Arabia, and returned once more to Damascus. (Galatians 1:11–17)

There is much in Paul's teaching that does reflect the authentic spirit of Judaism and Christianity as expressed in the Prime Directives and Jesus' gospel of mercy. But there is also much that does not, as we have seen in his comments on women, slavery, obedience to tyrannical governments, and the loutish nature of Cretans. Sadly, Paul's teachings on animals fall into the latter category.

In the Spirit of Aristotle

Paul's teachings about animals come out of his Greek, rather than his Jewish, background. We have seen that the Hebrew Scriptures teach that all of creation is sacred to God and must be treated with love, compassion, and respect. The most influential Greek philosophers taught that animals are simply resources for human use and are not entitled to moral consideration. We can treat them however we like with a clear conscience.[14] This theory is most baldly stated by Aristotle (383–322 BCE). In his treatise on social organization, Aristotle observes that human beings both eat animals and use them in various ways to earn a living. Then he claims that "Accordingly, if nature makes nothing purposeless or in vain [which is an axiom of Aristotelian philosophy], all animals must have been made by nature for the sake of man."[15] In other words, Aristotle assumes in this situation that because something *is*, it *is right*. This is always an attractive notion to those who possess wealth or power, because it justifies their privileged position in the world. It is, in fact, not an ethical statement at all, but an assertion that we do not need to concern ourselves with ethics, because a "higher power"—in this case, "nature"—has already arranged the world into an ethical order. All we have to do is accept the way things are and not make trouble for those at the top of the hierarchy.

Aristotle grew up in the palace of King Amyntas II of Macedonia, a small kingdom on the northern fringe of the Greek world, in the region now known as the Balkans. His father was court physician, and Aristotle was raised in close company with the royal family. Amyntas was succeeded on the throne by his son Philip, who subsequently employed Aristotle to educate his own son—the future Alexander the Great. The philosopher and the world-conquerer remained friends for life. Alexander sent back to his old tutor exotic animals from the faraway places he conquered, which Aristotle kept in the largest menagerie the classical world would know until the Romans began collecting vast numbers of African animals for slaughter in the Coliseum.

When Alexander died at thirty-two, Aristotle retired from public life and passed away the following year.

Reflecting the outlook of his royal friends and patrons, Aristotle taught that slaves exist to serve free men, women to serve men, barbarians to serve Greeks, and subjects to serve their rulers. Wherever we find a moral hierarchy—the notion that some beings are more worthy than others, and more deserving of moral consideration—we also find that it parallels the hierarchy of power in the surrounding world. Moral hierarchies of the sort created by Aristotle exist to defend the privileged position of those who possess power. They are rationalizations invented to justify the benefits that the powerful gain by oppressing the weak. They are the antithesis of the Prime Directives and the Hierarchy of Service.

Like Aristotle, Paul defended the dominance of men over women, free men over slaves, rulers over the ruled, and humans over animals. All he had to do was substitute "God" for "nature." And so, in deciding that God has no concern for animals, and therefore we need have none, Paul rejected both his Jewish background and the teachings of Jesus in favor of his Greek background. Jesus defended the poor and the downtrodden; Paul defended the aristocrats and rulers. Jesus said "the last shall be first"; Paul said the last shall obey the first. Jesus praised Mary, the sister of Martha and Lazarus, for wanting to discuss religion instead of attending to household chores (Luke 10:38–42); Paul told women to keep their heads covered and their mouths shut in church. Jesus liberated animals about to be sacrificed; Paul said God does not care what happens to animals. With the possible exception of fish, Jesus was a vegetarian; Paul told people to eat every kind of meat with a clear conscience.

Born to Die

Paul is not the only New Testament writer who absorbed the Aristotelian view of animals. In 2 Peter, we read about sinful Christians who are so brazen that "they do not tremble when they revile angelic majesties," whatever that may mean. (2 Peter 2:10) The author goes on to compare these sinners—in the English of the NASB—to "unreasoning animals, born as creatures of instinct to be captured and killed." (2 Peter 2:12)

Christian defenders of animal exploitation often assume that "born as creatures of instinct to be captured and killed" means "captured and killed by human beings for food, clothing, and so forth." But when we examine the passage closely, there is nothing in it to support this interpretation. The Greek word that the NASB translates "as creatures of instinct" is *physica*, which simply means "inborn," or "by nature."[16] It is the English translators who have assumed that "instinct" is the nature of animals. But the idea that animals are governed by mindless instinct is of relatively recent origin, being derived from the notion of the French philosopher René Descartes (1596–1650) that animals are mindless robots who can neither think nor feel. Aristotle had taught that animals have what he called a "sensitive soul," which is capable of both feeling and practical thought (i.e., day-to-day problem solving: figuring out ways to get food, to escape from danger, etc.). For Aristotle, what distinguished animals from humans was that the former were incapable of abstract thought of the sort we engage in when we ask questions like, "What is the meaning of life?" or "Why does the sun set in the west?" Thus, when the author of 2 Peter speaks of "unreasoning animals" (*aloga zoa*), he is simply reflecting the Greek view that animals are incapable of abstract reasoning; he is not saying that they are incapable of all thought.

Translated literally, and stripped of its post-Cartesian bias, the phrase we quoted above means "unreasoning animals by nature born to capture and death." In their wild or natural state—"in the course of nature," as the New English Bible's rendering of this verse so elegantly phrases it—animals capture and kill one another on a daily basis. That is a fact. And this passage in 2 Peter is nothing more than an acknowledgment of that fact. The author's point is that just as animals living in the wild are doomed by their physical and mental nature to be caught and killed by animals who are stronger, faster, or cleverer than they, so the souls of sinners who "revile angelic majesties" are condemned to death by their own sinful nature.

In the epistle of Jude, we find the same thought expressed in nearly identical language. Referring to people who "revile angelic majesties," the author says, "But these men revile the things which they do not understand; and the things which they know by instinct, like unreasoning animals, by these things they are destroyed." (Jude 10)

The Greek word that the NASB translates "by instinct" here is *physicos*, an adverbial form of *physica*.[7] It might more precisely be rendered "naturally," "by nature," or "according to their natures." The writer is saying that sinners have spiritual natures that condemn them to death by divine judgement, just as animals have physical and mental natures that condemn them to death by predation. As a result of the Greek culture they have absorbed, the authors of both Jude and 2 Peter believe that "reason" (i.e., the ability to reason abstractly) is the unique property of humankind—hence their use of the term "unreasoning animals"—but they do not condemn other species to mindless "instinct," as do most modern translators.

The point of both passages is the same. Those who "revile angelic majesties" will experience death as a consequence of their sinful natures, just as animals in the wild experience death as a consequence of not being physically or mentally equipped to escape their predators. It is a bizarre argument, but not one that provides support to the notion that we are entitled to kill animals for our own use.

* * *

Aristotle's doctrine of the moral hierarchy has been overturned in all of its applications except one. No Christian would any longer use it to defend slavery, assert the inferiority of women, or claim that Hitler and Stalin were "God's ministers" and the instruments of God's revenge on sinners, as Paul contended. In those cases, everyone recognizes that the hierarchy violates the Prime Directives and cannot be reconciled with the Gospel of Mercy. Only the exploitation of animals remains. It is time for us to discard this last remaining vestige of a discredited theory.

Notes

1. In 1 Timothy 5:17–18, Paul quotes the same verse and gives it the same interpretation.
2. Wesley, p. 1. As before, he is quoting from the KJV.
3. Strong number 3843. Thayer, p. 476.
4. Acts 9:11, 21:39, and 22:3.
5. Acts 22:3.
6. Acts 7:58, 8:1, 9:1–2.
7. Acts 22:25–29.
8. Strong number 4773. Thayer, p. 592.
9. Paul's Greek phrase is *Kaisaros oikias*. It is sometimes argued that "Caesar's household" refers to slaves in the service of the imperial family, and that is possible. But the term "household" was commonly used to mean "family." See Thayer, p. 439.
10. Acts 7:58, 8:1, 9:1–2.
11. Acts 9:3–22.
12. Galatians 2:8.

13. See, for example, Galatians 3. When Paul says, as he often does, that we are saved by "faith" and not "works" (e.g., Galatians 2:16), he means that we attain salvation by believing that Christ died for our sins, not by keeping the Jewish law.

14. There were, however, exceptions, the most important of whom was Pythagoras of Samos (flourished around 530 BCE), best known today for the Pythagorean theorem in geometry. Pythagoras taught that animals have souls identical to ours; he opposed animal sacrifice and advocated vegetarianism. From ancient times until the mid-nineteenth century, a vegetarian diet was known as a "Pythagorean diet."

15. Aristotle, *Politics*, Book I, Chapter 8.

16. Strong number 5446. Thayer, p. 660.

17. Strong number 5447. Thayer, p. 660.

15: Eat Anything You Want

P aul was unabashed in his endorsement of meat eating, including meat that was not kosher or had been dedicated to pagan gods. This was part and parcel of his strategy to attract gentile converts by not subjecting them to the restrictions of Jewish law. As a member of an aristocratic family with connections to the Greek city of Tarsus, Paul had been raised in a cosmopolitan atmosphere in which this multitude of regulations was not taken terribly seriously, and so he could jettison them with an easy conscience. In Colossians 2:16, he instructs gentile Christians not to let anyone criticize their choice of food and drink. Presumably he is referring to meat and alcohol. In 1 Timothy 4:1–4, he warns against "the hypocrisy of liars . . . who forbid marriage *and advocate* abstaining from foods which God has created to be gratefully shared in by those who believe and know the truth." Again we may presume that he is talking about meat. And finally, in 1 Corinthians 10:25–31, he tells his gentile converts, "Eat anything that is sold in the meat market without asking questions for conscience' sake; FOR THE EARTH IS THE LORD'S, AND ALL THAT IT CONTAINS. [Psalm 24:1; see also Psalm 50:12] If one of the unbelievers invites you and you want to go, eat anything that is set before you without asking questions for conscience' sake. But if anyone says to you, 'This is meat sacrificed to idols,' do not eat it, for the sake of the one who informed *you*, and for conscience' sake; I mean not your own conscience, but the other *man's*."

In each instance, the claims Paul is rebutting have nothing to do with the ethics of raising and slaughtering animals for food. That issue is not even on Paul's radar screen. As he makes clear in the last verses I quoted, he is worried about Jewish Christians who are trying to convince his gentile converts that they must not eat meat that has been offered to pagan gods, because to do so would be tantamount to idolatry.

The problem was that in the ancient world, especially in the cities, it was difficult to get meat that had not been offered to pagan deities. The temples of the various gods and goddesses had what amounted to a monopoly on the slaughter of animals. They raised the animals themselves, bought them from farmers, or accepted them from citizens who wanted a sacrifice offered on their own behalf. In either case, the priests slaughtered the animals, offered a small portion of the carcass as a sacrifice to the Temple's patron deity, and sold the rest of the meat, either retail or to butcher shops. Unless you bought your meat at a kosher butcher shop operated by Jews or made the arduous trip out of town to buy a living animal from a farmer, the odds were that it had been offered to a pagan deity.

Christians with "Weak Faith"

In 1 Corinthians 8, Paul discusses this issue at great length and with great vehemence. His logic is dense and convoluted, but essentially he argues that if your Christian faith is still weak enough that you are not entirely certain that the pagan deities are fictitious, then you are committing idolatry when you eat meat that has been dedicated to them. But if your Christian faith is so strong that you are absolutely certain the pagan deities are fictional creations, you can eat the meat with a clear conscience; you cannot worship what you know does not exist.

Nevertheless, toward the end of the chapter, Paul suggests that even Christians with strong faith may want to abstain from eating meat offered to pagan deities if there is any chance that their example will tempt fellow Christians of weaker faith into inadvertent idolatry. He concludes by saying, "Therefore, if food causes my brother to stumble, I will never eat meat again, so that I will not cause my brother to stumble." (1 Corinthians 8:13)

Some vegetarian and animal rights advocates have seized on this verse to claim Paul as a vegetarian. Sadly, I believe they are mistaken. This verse, I think, is nothing more than a rhetorical flourish intended to lend emphasis to Paul's point. There are no indications in Acts or Paul's letters that he ever followed through and actually became a vegetarian. No doubt he abstained from meat offered to pagan deities in the presence of Christians whose faith was still "weak." That would have been entirely in character for him. But there is no reason to think that he ever did more. But even if he did become a vegetarian, he did so not out of love and compassion for the slaughtered animals, but over an arcane religious issue peculiar to his place and time.

A Matter of Choice

Even so, Paul is not quite as hostile to vegetarianism as some defenders of meat eating claim. In discussing various kinds of spiritual weakness, Paul says, "One person has faith that he may eat all things, but he who is weak eats vegetables *only*." (Romans 14:2) Opponents of vegetarianism and animal rights sometimes read this verse to mean that vegetarianism is a sign of weak Christian faith, and that a good Christian cannot be a vegetarian. But that is not what Paul is saying. We have already seen that when Paul talks about "weak" faith in connection with meat eating, he is actually referring to eating meat that has been offered to idols, and that is what he is talking about in this letter, which was addressed to Christians living in Rome.

Around 50 CE, the Roman Emperor Claudius issued an edict banning Jews from the city of Rome, apparently because he suspected them of stirring up trouble on behalf of the Judean independence movement.¹ (As we might expect, the ban does not appear to have been applied to the Herods. Presumably, it exempted the small number of Jews who were Roman citizens.) Jews continued to live in Rome, but they had much the same status as undocumented aliens in the United States. They had to keep a low profile and avoid coming to the attention of the authorities. Being in the city illegally, Jews could not operate kosher butcher shops for fear of being turned in by pagan butchers anxious to eliminate the competition. Therefore, it was next to impossible in Rome to obtain meat that had not been offered to a pagan deity. The "weak" who "eat only vegetables" are the same "weak" that Paul discussed in 1 Corinthians chapter 8. But in Rome, they have to avoid all meat, because there is none available that has not been offered to pagan deities. With this background, we can see that *although Paul did not support vegetarianism, he did not condemn it, either*. As he says in Romans 14:3, "The one who eats is not to regard with contempt the one who does not eat, and the one who does not eat is not to judge the one who eats, for God has accepted him." To Paul, eating meat, even meat offered to idols, was a personal choice and not an ethical or spiritual issue. With the caveat against leading a "weaker neighbor" into idolatry, his view was that a Christian could adopt it or reject it with an equally clear conscience.

Defenders of all forms of animal abuse, including animal agriculture, fur, and hunting and fishing, are increasingly adopting Paul's position by claiming that these are matters of personal choice. They generously agree that animal advocates should be free not to eat meat, wear leather or fur, or hunt and fish. On the other hand, they argue, it is only fair that others should be equally free to engage in those activities if they wish.

They are wrong. Tormenting and killing God's sensitive living souls is not an ethically neutral personal choice. It is a quintessentially ethical and spiritual question whose answer is dictated by the Prime Directives. We have no moral right to make choices that destroy the happiness and steal the lives of helpless beings who are absolutely at our mercy. When Paul tells us otherwise, he is transmitting views acquired from his aristocratic Greco-Roman background, views that he found immensely helpful in attracting gentile converts.

"The Greatest of These Is Love"

So far, we have been focusing on the static in Paul's teachings, but at other times, Paul expresses the spirit of the Prime Directives with a clarity and purity that are breathtaking. His assertions, for example, that all of the created universe will experience salvation and participate in the kingdom of heaven reflect a vision of divine love and mercy that is all-encompassing and excludes no being from its blessing.

The essence of the Prime Directives is love, universal, all-pervasive love. Paul has expressed this love in one of the most profound and moving passages in all the spiritual literature of the world, the well-known and deeply cherished thirteenth chapter of 1 Corinthians. I will quote it here in the familiar and beautiful King James Version, except that I have substituted "love" for "charity," which has lost this meaning in modern English.

> Though I speak with the tongues of men and of angels, and have not love, I am become as sounding brass, or a tinkling cymbal. And though I have the gift of prophecy, and understand all mysteries, and all knowledge; and though I have all faith, so that I could remove mountains, and have not love, I am nothing. And though I

bestow all my goods to feed the poor, and though I give my body to be burned, and have not love, it profiteth me nothing. Love suffereth long, and is kind; love envieth not; love vaunteth not itself, is not puffed up, doth not behave itself unseemly, seeketh not her own, is not easily provoked, thinketh no evil; rejoiceth not in iniquity, but rejoiceth in the truth; beareth all things, believeth all things, hopeth all things, endureth all things. Love never faileth: but whether there be prophecies, they shall fail; whether there be tongues, they shall cease; whether there be knowledge, it shall vanish away. For we know in part, and we prophesy in part. But when that which is perfect is come, then that which is in part shall be done away. When I was a child, I spake as a child, I understood as a child, I thought as a child; but when I became a man, I put away childish things. For now we see through a glass, darkly; but then face to face: now I know in part; but then shall I know even as also I am known. And now abideth faith, hope, love, these three; but the greatest of these is love.

Paul saw clearly the primacy of love, even if sometimes he saw how to practice that love "through a glass, darkly." He got the fundamental principle exactly right, even as his background and his mission kept him from seeing how that principle applies to women, slaves, homosexuals, victims of tyranny, and animals. This task of working out the application of fundamental spiritual truths to concrete situations is never-ending. It is not left to the writers of Scripture alone; it falls to each and every one of us. It is the challenge of the religious life. We have been given the Prime Directives, but we are responsible for putting them into practice in our own lives. This is a difficult task, filled with uncertainties and ambiguities, and there is much that people of good conscience can disagree over. But one thing is clear. The Prime Directives do not authorize the eternal Treblinka, and we who would try to live by them as closely as we are able must give up living off the suffering and death of its inmates.

Notes

1. Acts 18:2; Suetonius, *The Lives of the Twelve Caesars*, "Claudius," 25.

Conclusion: The Dominion of Love

When this book was well underway, but before I had a title in mind, I took part in a panel discussion on religion and animal rights. During a question-and-answer period, a young man in the audience told us that he often went into Christian chat rooms on the internet and started discussions about animal rights. "When they come back at me with 'dominion,' " he told us, "I ask them, 'If God's dominion is love, and a king's dominion is stewardship, why should humanity's dominion be torture, abuse, and killing?' " When the session ended, several people came up to talk with the speakers, and the young man left before I could catch up with him. I don't know his name or where he lives. But he had framed the issue of dominion in a more precise and elegant way than I had ever heard, and he had given me the title I had been looking for.

"The dominion of love" sounds like one of those grandiloquent but vacuous phrases that give the impression of great profundity while meaning nothing at all. But it is not. The dominion of love is concrete, practical, and down-to-earth; there is nothing grandiose about it. It is not something to be pursued only by saints, holy men and women, or advanced spiritual pilgrims. It involves no special skills, no hidden knowledge, no ordinations or long courses of study, and no mystical or esoteric practices. The dominion of love is nothing more complicated than the way we make the dozens of mundane decisions that shape our daily lives.

We exercise the dominion of love when we adopt a companion animal from a shelter instead of buying from a breeder or pet store.

We exercise the dominion of love when we spay or neuter our companion animals to assure that no additional dogs or cats come into the world while millions are being killed every year because there are no homes for them.

We exercise the dominion of love when we give up hunting and fishing and when we post our land so that no one else can turn it into a killing ground.

We exercise the dominion of love when we refuse to become tourists at animal concentration camps, such as zoos and circuses with animal acts.

We exercise the dominion of love when we drive more slowly and carefully at dusk and after dark to lessen the chance of hitting a frightened animal who may dart across the road in our headlights.

We exercise the dominion of love when we learn to share the space that we call "ours" with others who may depend on it for their lives. We allow the deer, rabbits, raccoons, opossums, and moles to browse in our gardens and dig their tunnels under our lawns, and we do not set out traps or poisons; we have no right to turn eating into a capital offense.

We exercise the dominion of love when we secure our homes to exclude mice, bats, squirrels, and other critters rather than carelessly letting them find a way in and then killing or "relocating" them after they have set up housekeeping. (Some "relocation" services simply kill the animals once they are out of our sight. It's quicker and cheaper.)

We exercise the dominion of love when we speak out against the eternal Treblinka in which our society imprisons animals: when we write a letter to the editor; when we volunteer our time or contribute money to a group that is working for animal protection; when we call a radio talk show and describe the suffering of animals in laboratories; when we pass out leaflets that depict the suffering of animals in circuses; and when we request that luncheons and dinners sponsored by groups at our synagogue or church not include the bodies of our murdered neighbors. The animals cannot speak on their own behalf; they cannot picket or demonstrate; they cannot vote, and they cannot contribute to political campaigns. They are counting on us to be their voice. Every time we speak out for them, we practice the dominion of love.

We exercise the dominion of love when we buy household and personal products that contain no animal ingredients and have not been tested on animals.

Most of all, we exercise the dominion of love when we decide that no living being will have to be imprisoned and killed to make our food and clothing. We don't eat meat, eggs, dairy products, or honey. We don't wear fur, leather, wool, or silk. This requires a little retraining—we have to find the stores and internet sites that sell comfortable and attractive non-leather shoes; we have to develop some new grocery shopping habits—but we don't have to do it all at once. I was a vegetarian for over a year before I became a vegan by ridding my life of milk, eggs, cheese, leather, wool, and silk. What matters is that we take the first steps and continue moving in the right direction. In modern American society, no one can live as a perfect vegan, but we can all do our best, and we can always try to do better today than we did yesterday. Adopting a cruelty-free lifestyle is not painful, not difficult, and does not empty our lives of pleasure. Quite the opposite, it fills our lives with joy. Eating and dressing, which used to be meaningless acts, are now filled with profound meaning. Every time we sit down to a vegetarian meal, every time we put on a pair of non-leather shoes, we save lives; we refuse to contribute to the world's store of suffering, and by so doing we lessen it. *There is nothing that you and I can do that will ease the suffering of animals more than refusing to eat their bodies or wear their skins.* It is the most important step that we can take to exercise the dominion of love.

* * *

There is a scene in the movie *Schindler's List* in which the sadistic commander of the concentration camp reminds Oskar Schindler that as Commandant he has the power to kill any and every prisoner in the camp. Schindler replies that when one has the power of life and death, the person who does not kill actually exercises greater power than the person who kills. Schindler was telling the Commandant that resisting Lord Acton's corruption of power requires great strength of character, while exercising power selfishly, indulgently, and wantonly is a sign of weakness. Amon Goeth, the Commandant of Schindler's camp, had been corrupted by his power over the prisoners in the same way that we have been corrupted by our power over the animals. It is time for us to earn the pride that theologians and philosophers express in our status as beings who are able to make moral choices. It is time we began actually making moral choices instead of inventing clever excuses for not making them. It is time we showed a little backbone. It is time we liberated our prisoners.

Appendix 1: Biblical Verses Relating to Human Treatment of Animals

Animals Possess Intelligence and Emotions

Genesis 9:2—Animals can experience "fear and terror."

Deuteronomy 25:4—"You shall not muzzle the ox while he is threshing." This presumes that the ox can experience both the physical distress of hunger and the emotional distress of being tantalized by food that he cannot have.

Psalm 104:29—Animals are "dismayed" (KJV "troubled") when God does not provide for them.

Proverbs 30: 24–28—Animals ranging from ants to lizards to locusts are "exceedingly wise" because they are capable of social organization and cooperative labor.

Isaiah 1:3—An ox can recognize his owner and a donkey can find his owner's manger.

Jeremiah 8:7—Storks, doves, and other birds have intelligence and understanding suited to their way of life.

Joel 1:18—Cattle, oxen, and sheep were suffering because of a drought.

Joel 2:22—God tells the cattle in the field not to be afraid.

Luke 13:34—Jesus cites a mother hen with her chicks as an example of selfless concern for the welfare of others.

Animals Possess Souls

Genesis 1:21—God created "every living soul that moves" in the water.

Genesis 1:24—God said "Let the earth bring forth every living soul according to his own nature, cattle, and crawling things, and animals."

Genesis 2:7 & 19—God created humankind and animals with the same "living soul." (In Hebrew *nephesh chayah*, in both cases, although English translations often obscure what is clear in the original text.)

Genesis 9:10—The animals who were in the ark with Noah are described as "living souls."

Leviticus 11:10—Shellfish and crustaceans are described as "living souls."

See *Covenant with the Animals* and *Heaven/Life after Death*

Bal Taschit ("Not Destroying," the Rabbinic Principle of Protecting the Environment)

Deuteronomy 20:19–20—Instructions not to destroy fruit trees in time of war. This is the Biblical injunction that forms the primary basis for the teachings on *bal taschit.*

Cats

Cats are not mentioned in the Bible.

Clean and Unclean Animals

See *Kashrut.*

Cleansing of the Temple

John 2:14–16—Jesus drove the money-changers and live animal dealers from the courtyard of the Temple in history's first recorded direct action in support of animal liberation. Also, Matthew 21:12–13; Mark 11:15–17; Luke 19:45–46.

Clothing

Genesis 3:21—God provided Adam and Eve with clothes made from animal skins.

2 Kings 1:8—The prophet Elijah is described as wearing a leather girdle about his waist.

Matthew 3:4—John the Baptist wore a garment of camel's hair and a leather belt. Also Mark 1:6.

Companions

Genesis 2:18–19—Animals were created as companions for humankind.

Covenants with the Animals

Genesis 9:8–17—After the flood, God established "an everlasting covenant" with "every living thing of every kind," that never again "shall there be a flood to lay waste the earth."

Hosea 2:18—God promises to make a covenant with "the wild animals, the birds of the air, and the things that crawl on the earth" that some day there will be an age without war so that all living creatures may "lie down in safety."

Dogs

Matthew 7:6—Jesus said not to give dogs what is holy or drop pearls in front of pigs. Apparently by "dogs" and "pigs," Jesus meant "gentiles." See Matthew 15:21–28, where he straightforwardly refers to gentiles as "dogs," and Acts 10, where "unclean" animals, such as pigs, represent gentiles in Peter's vision.

Matthew 15:21–28—Jesus said that it is not right to take the children's food and give it to dogs, by which he meant that it was not right to give to gentiles blessings meant for Jews. Also Mark 7:24–30.

Philippians 3:2—Paul refers to his opponents as "dogs" and "evil workers." Paul is probably being deliberately insulting by using a common term for male prostitutes. See the listing for Revelation 22:15, immediately below.

Revelation 22:15—Uses the Greek word for "dog" (*kyon*, Strong number 2965) to mean "male prostitute," apparently in keeping with common Jewish usage going back hundreds of years. See Deuteronomy 23:18, which uses the Hebrew word for "dog" (*keleb*, Strong number 3611) in the same way.

Dominion

Genesis 1:28—Humankind has dominion over every living being. See also Psalm 8:5–8.

Psalm 23—A description of how humanity's dominion ought to be exercised.

Psalm 36:6—God saves humans and animals alike.

Psalm 84:3—Birds are welcome to build their nests on God's altar.

Psalm 104:10–30—God fashioned the world in ways that provide for the needs of humans and animals alike.

Psalm 145:14–16—God's dominion over both humankind and animals is to sustain those who fall and feed those who are hungry.

Matthew 6:26—Jesus said that God provides for the "birds of the air."

Matthew 10:29—Jesus said that God is concerned not just for human beings, but even for tiny sparrows. See also Luke 12:6.

John 10:11–15—Jesus described himself as "the good shepherd" who is willing to die for his sheep.

Fish/Fishing/Fishers

Matthew 4:18–22—With the words "I will make you fishers of people," Jesus called two sets of brothers, Simon Peter and Andrew, and James and John bar Zebedee, from their work as commercial fishers to be his disciples. "Immediately they left their nets and followed him." Also Mark 1:16–20, and Luke 5:1–11. Luke contradicts Matthew and Mark by having Jesus miraculously help the brothers fill their nets with fish before they leave to become his disciples.

Matthew 7:9–11—Jesus asked rhetorically if any father would give his son a stone when the child asked for a fish. Also Luke 11:11–13.

Matthew 14:13–21—"The Feeding of the Five Thousand." Jesus miraculously multiplied five rolls and two fish into enough to feed "five thousand men, to say nothing of the women and children." Also Mark 6:34–44, Luke 9:10–17, and John 6:3–13.

Matthew 15:32–38—"The Feeding of the Four Thousand." Jesus miraculously multiplied seven rolls and "a few small fish" into enough to feed "four thousand men, besides women and children." Also Mark 8:1–9.

Matthew 17:24–27—Jesus told Simon Peter to throw a line into the water and catch a fish, in whose mouth he would find a coin with which they could pay the Temple tax. It is not recorded whether Peter actually did this.

Luke 24:33–43—The resurrected Jesus accepted a piece of fish from his disciples and ate it to prove to them that he was not a ghost.

John 21:1–14—The resurrected Jesus appeared to his disciples, who were fishing in the Sea of Galilee. He miraculously helped them catch a net full of fish, cooked some fish, and offered it to them for breakfast.

Food

Proverbs 15:17—"Better is a dish of vegetables where love is than a fattened ox *served* with hatred." Proverbs is traditionally held to have been written by King Solomon, who lived an opulent lifestyle, ate meat, and sacrificed vast numbers of animals.

Matthew 3:4—John the Baptist lived on a diet of "locusts and wild honey," or, as some scholars read the ancient text, "cakes dipped in wild honey." See also Mark 1:6.

Matthew 15:1–20—When some Pharisees accuse Jesus of allowing his disciples to eat without washing their hands as required by Jewish law, he replies that what goes into a person's mouth cannot defile him; only his thoughts and deeds can defile him. Also Mark 7:1–23.

Luke 7:33–34—Jesus remarks that because "John the Baptist came eating no bread and drinking no wine," people said he was crazy, while Jesus does not follow John's ascetic diet and people call him a glutton and a drunk. Also Matthew 11:18–19.

1 Corinthians 8—Paul tells Christians they may eat "things" and "food" (which would include meat) that have been offered to pagan deities unless their doing so will tempt a fellow Christian into idolatry.

Colossians 2:16—Paul tells Christians not to let anyone criticize them for what they eat or drink.

1 Timothy 4:1–5—Paul condemns "hypocrites" who advocate abstaining from certain foods, presumably meat, because "everything that God created is good, and nothing is to be rejected if it is received with gratitude."

See also *Kashrut, Meat Eating,* and *Vegetarianism.*

Gadarene Pigs

Matthew 8:28–34—Jesus exorcised demons from a man who lived near the town of Gadara and gave them permission to enter the bodies of pigs who were foraging nearby. The pigs, about two thousand in number, went insane, ran into the Sea of Galilee, and drowned. Also Mark 5:1–19 and Luke 8:26–39.

Hair and Skins of Animals

Exodus 25:5—God instructed Moses to take up a collection for the building of a large portable shrine (known as the Tabernacle). Among the donations that could be accepted were animals' hair and skins. The use of animal hair and skins on the Tabernacle is further described in Exodus 26:7, 26:14, 35:7, 35:23, 36:19, 39:34; Numbers 4:6, 8, 10, 11, 12, 14, and 25.

Heaven/Life after Death/The Messianic Era

Ecclesiastes 3:19–21—Human beings and animals, having the same living spirit, share the same fate at death, which the author viewed as most likely oblivion.

Isaiah 11:6–9—"The Peaceable Kingdom." Animals will be present in the Kingdom of Heaven and will live together in harmony with each other and with humankind.

Hosea 2:18—Animals will be present in the Kingdom of Heaven, and humans will no longer prey upon them.

Romans 8:19–22—Paul affirms that "the whole created universe" will share in salvation.

Ephesians 1:9–10—Paul states that the entire universe, "all in heaven and on earth," will be "brought into unity with Christ."

Colossians 1:19–20—Paul says that through Christ "God chose to reconcile the whole universe to himself . . . to reconcile all things, whether on earth or in heaven, through him alone."

Hunting

Genesis 10:8–9—Nimrod was "a mighty hunter before the Lord." Since he was the king of Babel, the Jewish tradition regards Nimrod's hunting as a sign of his rebelliousness against God, a rebelliousness demonstrated in the construction of the infamous Tower of Babel. (See Genesis 10:10 and 11:1–9.)

Genesis 25:27—Isaac's son Esau, "became a skillful hunter, a man of the field, but Jacob [his brother] was a peaceful man, living in tents." Esau is depicted in Genesis as rebellious, vengeful, and lacking in judgment. It was his peaceful brother, Jacob, who became the ancestor of the Jewish nation.

Genesis 27:5—Esau goes out to hunt for deer.

Leviticus 17:13–14—Requires hunters to drain the blood of their victims and cover it with earth.

1 Samuel 26:20—David pleads with Saul not to hunt him down and kill him "just as one hunts a partridge in the mountains."

Proverbs 12:27—"A lazy man does not catch his prey."

Image of God

Genesis 1:26–27—Humankind was created in God's image. See also Genesis 9:6.

Colossians 3:9–10—A Christian's new nature is being constantly renewed in the image of its creator. This suggests that the image of God resides in our hearts and in our behavior rather than in our appearance.

Kashrut (Dietary Laws)

Genesis 9:4—Instructions not to eat anything with the blood still in it. Also Leviticus 19:26 and Deuteronomy 12:16 & 23–25.

Exodus 23:19—Instructions not to cook a kid in his mother's milk. This is the Biblical basis for the requirement not to eat milk and meat in the same meal. Also Deuteronomy 14:21.

Leviticus 11—Instructions concerning which animals may and may not be eaten. Also Deuteronomy 14:3–20.

Deuteronomy 14:21—Instructions that the flesh of an animal that has died of natural causes may not be eaten.

Kindness to Animals Required

Genesis 49:6–7—God was angry with Israel for killing men and crippling oxen.

Exodus 23: 4–5—Instructions that one must return an enemy's ox who is lost and free an enemy's donkey who has fallen beneath his burden, indicating a direct moral duty to animals that is more important than our strongest passions.

Exodus 23:10–11—Every seventh year, fields must be left fallow to provide food for the poor and for wildlife.

Exodus 23:12—Instructions that animals must be allowed to rest on the sabbath. (Also in the Ten Commandments: Exodus 20:8–11 and Deuteronomy 5:12–15.)

Numbers 22:21–34—Guidance that it is sinful to mistreat an animal. (The story of Balaam, who mistreated his donkey and was reprimanded by an angel.)

Deuteronomy 22:1–3—Instructions to care for lost animals and return them to their owner.

Deuteronomy 22:4—Instructions to help a working animal who has fallen beneath his burden.

Deuteronomy 22:6—Instructions not to take both the mother bird and the eggs from the nest.

Deuteronomy 22:10—Instructions not to plow with an ox and a donkey yoked together. (This puts too great a strain on the donkey.)

Deuteronomy 25:4—Instructions not to muzzle an ox while he is threshing.

Proverbs 12:10—"A righteous man has regard for the life of his animal, But *even* the compassion of the wicked is cruel." This is a specific statement that we have direct moral obligations to animals.

Habakkuk 2:17—God told the Jews that their terrorizing of animals in Lebanon during a recent war was a crime that will "overwhelm" them.

Luke 13:15—Jesus noted with approval that everyone who owns an ox or a donkey works on the sabbath in order to give the animal water.

Luke 14:5—Jesus endorsed the Jewish teaching that there is a moral duty to break the sabbath to help an animal in distress. (Indicating a direct moral duty to animals that overrides other religious obligations.)

Kindness to Animals Not Required

1 Corinthians 9:9–10—Paul says that God does not care about animals, directly contradicting the Jewish teachings on *tsar ba'ale hayim* and the teachings of Jesus. See also 1 Timothy 5:17–18.

Meat Eating

Genesis 9:1–3—God gave Noah and his descendents permission to eat "every living thing." This passage specifically states that it is rescinding the vegan diet required by Genesis 1:29.

Genesis 18:1–8—God, accompanied by two angels, visited Abraham in human form. Abraham slaughtered a calf for them, which they ate.

Numbers 11—During the exodus, the people of Israel insisted on having meat to eat. God provided them with quail, then punished them with a plague.

Deuteronomy 12:20–22—God gave the people of Israel permission to eat meat in locations other than those where animals may be sacrificed if they had a craving for it. (See Deuteronomy 12:5–7, which limits sacrifice to places specifically designated by God.)

1 Samuel 14:32–35—The people of Israel slaughtered and ate oxen and bulls. King Saul built an emergency altar so the people would not eat the meat with the blood still in it. See Genesis 9:4–5.

1 Corinthians 10:25–31—Paul tells Christians they may eat whatever is sold in the meat markets without any qualms of conscience. See also *Food*.

Sacrifice of Animals Said to Be Approved by God

Genesis 4:3–5—God preferred Abel's sacrifice of animals to Cain's offering of "the fruit of the ground" (i.e., plants; whether grain; fruits or vegetables we are not told).

Genesis 8:20–21—God approved of Noah's sacrifice of animals after the flood.

Genesis 22:1–14—God ordered Abraham to offer his son as a sacrifice, then provided him with a sacrificial ram instead.

1 Kings 8:5—King Solomon offered animal sacrifices "in numbers past counting" at the dedication of the Temple.

Psalm 4:5—The Psalmist says that one should offer sacrifices when worried or anxious.

Psalm 66:15—The Psalmist promises to offer sacrifices to God.

Luke 2:22–24—Following Jesus' birth, Mary and Joseph went to the Temple and sacrificed two doves or pigeons. The instructions for this sacrifice are given in Leviticus 12.

Sacrifice of Animals Said to Be Commanded by God

Exodus 12:3–11—Instructions for the sacrifice of lambs for Passover. Also Deuteronomy 16:1–8.

Exodus 29:1–35—Instructions for sacrifices in connection with the ordination of priests.

Exodus 29:36–42—Instructions for daily sacrifices.

Leviticus 1—Instructions for burnt offerings.

Leviticus 3—Instructions for the "peace offering."

Leviticus 4—Instructions for the sin offering.

Leviticus 7:1–8—Instructions for the guilt offering.

Leviticus 8–9—God instructed Moses and Aaron (Moses' brother, the first high priest) to offer sacrifices.

Leviticus 14: 10–32 & 48–53—Instructions for animal sacrifice as part of the ritual for curing leprosy.

Leviticus 15—Instructions for animal sacrifice as part of the ritual for curing various bodily discharges.

Leviticus 16—Instructions for animal sacrifice as part of the ritual of *Yom Kippur*, the Day of Atonement.

Leviticus 19:20–22—Instructions for a guilt offering for having sexual relations with someone else's slave.

Leviticus 22:17–30—Instructions for determining which animals are suitable for sacrifice.

Leviticus 23:16–21—Instructions for burnt offerings in conjunction with "holy convocations."

Numbers 6:9–21—Instructions for sacrificing animals in connection with a Nazirite vow.

Numbers 7—Description of animal sacrifices in connection with the consecration of the tabernacle.

Numbers 15:1–26—Instructions to the people of Israel for sacrificing animals when they entered the Promised Land following the exodus. Also Deuteronomy 27:4–7.

Numbers 28–29—Instructions for sacrificing animals in connection with various holy days.

Deuteronomy 12:5–6—Instructions to offer sacrifices only in the place designated by God. (This had the effect of reducing the number of sacrifices.)

Judges 13:16–20—An angel told Samson's father to offer an animal sacrifice and a grain offering to God.

Sacrifice of Animals Said to Be Condemned by God

1 Samuel 15:21–23—When King Saul prepared to offer animal sacrifices, God told him through the prophet Samuel that God preferred obedience to sacrifices.

Psalm 40:6—God does not desire sacrifices.

Isaiah 1:11–15—God says that sacrifices are disgusting, that God has never asked for sacrifices, and that God will not hear the prayers of people who offer sacrifices because their "hands are covered with blood."

Isaiah 66:3—God says that there is no difference between animal sacrifice and human sacrifice.

Jeremiah 7:21–23—God says that God did not command the sacrifices described in Exodus, Leviticus, Numbers, and Deuteronomy.

Hosea 6:6—God wants mercy and piety, not sacrifices.

Hosea 8:13—God tells the Jewish people that as punishment for offering sacrifices, they will go back into slavery.

Amos 5:21–25—God condemns sacrifices and says that the people of Israel did not offer the sacrifices described in Exodus, Leviticus, Numbers, and Deuteronomy.

Micah 6:6–8—God does not want people to offer sacrifices. Instead, God wants them to simply "do justly, and to love mercy, and to walk humbly with your God."

Sacrifice of Animals in the New Testament

Matthew 9:13—Jesus condemned animal sacrifice.

Matthew 12:7—Jesus again condemned animal sacrifice.

Mark 1:40–45—Jesus told a leper whom he had cured to go to the Temple and offer the sacrifice appropriate to being cured of leprosy (see Leviticus 14). See also Matthew 8:2–4 and Luke 5:12–14.

Mark 12:28–34—A Jewish teacher told Jesus that love of God and neighbor is more important than sacrifices. Jesus told him he was "not far from the Kingdom of Heaven," meaning that he only needed to make the one further step of recognizing that sacrifices are not simply less important, but inherently wrong.

Hebrews 10:1–18—Animal sacrifices never accomplished their intended purpose because "it is impossible for the blood of bulls and goats to take away sins."

Triumphal Entry into Jerusalem

Matthew 21:1–11—As a crowd cheered, Jesus rode a donkey into Jerusalem to fulfill a prophecy (Zechariah 9:9) that the messiah would appear riding on a donkey. See also Mark 11:1–10, Luke 19:29–38, and John 12:12–15.

Tsar Ba'ale Hayim ("Suffering of Living Beings," the Rabbinical Doctrine That It Is Wrong to Cause Animals Suffering)

Deuteronomy 25:4—Instructions not to muzzle an ox while he is threshing. This is the primary Biblical foundation for *tsar ba'ale hayim.*

Vegetarianism/Veganism

Genesis 1:29–30—God commanded humankind to follow a vegan diet (*vee*-gun, containing no animal products of any kind). According to Genesis 9:3, this command was not rescinded after the expulsion from the Garden of Eden, but stayed in effect until after the flood.

Exodus 16, Numbers 11—During the exodus, the people of Israel complained that they did not have enough to eat, so God miraculously provided them with manna, a vegan food that sustained them for forty years. According to Numbers, they were unhappy with the vegan manna and insisted on meat, which angered God, who sent them quail that caused a plague that killed many of them.

Daniel 1:8–16—Daniel refused to eat the meat that the Babylonian king directed him to eat and insisted on vegetarian food. It is not clear whether Daniel objected to the King's meat because it was meat or because it was not kosher and had been dedicated to pagan gods.

Daniel 10:2–3—During a three-week meditation retreat seeking a vision from God, Daniel consumed "no rich food, no meat, and no wine," suggesting that his normal diet included meat.

Romans 14:2—Paul says that the weak Christian "eats vegetables only." He is referring to people who refuse to eat meat that has been dedicated to pagan deities because they still take those deities seriously enough to believe that eating the meat would constitute an act of pagan worship.

See also *Food.*

Appendix 2: Suggestions for Further Reading

Animal Agriculture

Davis, Karen, Ph.D., *Prisoned Chickens, Poisoned Eggs*. A well-researched and thoroughly documented description of modern poultry farming by the founder and president of United Poultry Concerns, a group dedicated to the protection of domestic fowl.

Eisnitz, Gail A., *Slaughterhouse: The Shocking Story of Greed, Neglect, and Inhumane Treatment Inside the U.S. Meat Industry*. Modern slaughterhouses as seen through the eyes of their employees.

Mason, Jim, and Peter Singer, *Animal Factories: What Agribusiness is Doing to the Family Farm, the Environment, and Your Health*. The classic exposé of modern animal agriculture.

Animal Consciousness, Emotions, and Intelligence

Barber, Theodore Xenophon, *The Human Nature of Birds: A Scientific Discovery with Startling Implications*. A well-written, well-documented look at the intelligence and emotions of animals.

Bekoff, Marc (editor), *The Smile of a Dolphin: Remarkable Accounts of Animal Emotions*. Brief but thought-provoking stories by scientists and researchers document the fresh look that many scientists are taking at animal consciousness and character.

Davis, Karen, Ph.D., *More Than a Meal: The Turkey in History, Myth, Ritual, and Reality*. At once scholarly and a good read, this is the definitive book on turkeys as sentient beings and cultural symbols.

Brilliantly demolishes the speciesist notion that only the "higher mammals" have a rich mental and emotional life.

Fouts, Roger, with Stephen Tukel Mills, *Next of Kin: My Conversations with Chimpanzees.* The fascinating story of chimpanzees who leaned to use American Sign Language to communicate with human beings.

Kowalski, Gary, *The Souls of Animals.* A brilliant and moving look at the personhood of nonhuman animals by a Unitarian-Universalist minister who concludes that "Animals, like us, are living souls. They are not things . . . With us they share in the gifts of consciousness and life. In a wonderful and inexpressible way, therefore, God is present in all creatures."

Kreisler, Kristin von, *The Compassion of Animals: True Stories of Animal Courage and Kindness.* Accounts of animals displaying love, devotion, compassion, self-sacrifice, and other "higher" emotions collected from around the world by a staff writer for *Reader's Digest.*

——. *Beauty in the Beasts: True Stories of Animals Who Choose to Do Good.* A worthy sequel to *The Compassion of Animals.*

Linden, Eugene, *The Parrot's Lament: And Other True Tales of Animal Intrigue, Intelligence, and Ingenuity.* An accessible, fascinating look at animal intelligence by a well-known science writer.

Masson, Jeffrey Moussaieff and Susan McCarthy, *When Elephants Weep: The Emotional Lives of Animals.* The well-documented, well-written book that made it respectable to talk about animals having emotions.

Randour, Mary Lou, Ph.D., *Animal Grace: Entering a Spiritual Relationship with Our Fellow Creatures.* An elegant, intelligent, and ecumenical meditation on animals, nonviolence, and the life of the spirit. Direct and personal, *Animal Grace* explores what human spiritual progress implies for our relationship with animals and *vice versa.*

Animal Protection and Religion

Akers, Keith, *The Lost Religion of Jesus: Simple Living and Nonviolence in Early Christianity.* A reconstruction from ancient sources of the religion actually taught by Jesus. Well written and solidly researched by an eminent vegetarian scholar, this is the most important book on the "historical Jesus" to appear since Albert Schweitzer's *The Quest for the Historical Jesus.*

Berry, Rynn, *Food for the Gods: Vegetarianism and the World's Religions.* A collection of essays by a highly respected vegetarian scholar on the attitude of nine different religious traditions, including Judaism, Catholicism, Eastern Orthodoxy, and Protestantism, toward animals and a vegetarian diet. Each essay is paired with an extended interview with a representative of the tradition. An elegantly written and informative work.

Hyland, J. R., *God's Covenant With Animals: A Biblical Basis for the Humane Treatment of All Creatures.* A groundbreaking examination of the Bible's attitude toward animals by an ordained evangelical minister. Focusing primarily on animal sacrifice, Reverend Hyland also touches on vegetarianism, hunting, fur and other issues. A reprint (with four additional chapters) of her earlier book *The Slaughter of Terrified Beasts* (Viatoris Ministries, 1988), which has become a classic in the literature of animal rights in the Judeo-Christian tradition.

Kalechofsky, Roberta, Ph.D. (editor), *Judaism and Animal Rights: Classical and Contemporary Responses.* A collection of forty-one essays by authors ranging from Temple Grandin, advisor to the meat industry on "humane" slaughter techniques, to Henry Spira, pioneering animal rights advocate. Among the most useful are contributions by Kalechofsky herself and Richard Schwartz. Dr. Kalechofsky and Professor Schwartz are eloquent and erudite proponents of vegetarianism and animal rights as expressions of Jewish faith and practice. Available from Micah Publications, 255 Humphrey Street, Marblehead, MA 01945.

——. *Vegetarian Judaism: A Guide for Everyone.* Although focusing primarily on religion and ethics, Dr. Kalechofsky also deals with issues of health and ecology. An extremely useful book for the Jewish vegetarian, it includes vegan versions of traditional Jewish recipes and a resource list. Available from Micah Publications, 255 Humphrey Street, Marblehead, MA 01945.

Kowalski, Gary, *The Bible According to Noah: Theology as if Animals Mattered*. Thought-provoking reflections on the Bible's portrayal of our relationship with animals, by a Unitarian-Universalist minister who believes that all of God's children matter.

Linzey, Andrew, *Christianity and the Rights of Animals*. This pioneering book has become the standard work on Christianity and animal protection. An Anglican priest and holder of the first post of Christian Theology and Animal Welfare at Mansfield College, Oxford University, Dr. Linzey is perhaps the world's best known Christian animal rights theologian.

———. *Animal Theology*. More technical than *Christianity and the Rights of Animals*, this is a systematic review of the issues and questions facing Christianity as a consequence of our exploitation of animals.

———. *Animal Gospel*. A wide-ranging discussion of animal rights as Christian service. Less formal and more personal than Linzey's previous books, *Animal Gospel* is a powerful call for Christians to end all exploitation of animals. The opening essay, "Overview: Gospel Truths about Animals," is the best brief introduction I have seen to animal rights from a Christian perspective.

Murti, Vasu, *"They Shall Not Hurt or Destroy": Moral and Theological Objections to the Human Exploitation of Nonhuman Animals*. Primarily an extensive and impressively researched commentary on Biblical and Christian writing in defense of animals, *They Shall Not Hurt or Destroy* also discusses abortion, war, and the death penalty (all of which Murti believes have much in common), and includes chapters on ancient Greece, Islam, and Baha'i. Published by its author, this is an important book that deserves to find a commercial publisher and a wider audience. Available from Vasu Murti, 30 Villanova Lane, Oakland, CA 94611.

Regenstein, Lewis G., *Replenish the Earth: A History of Organized Religion's Treatment of Animals and Nature: Including the Bible's Message of Conservation and Kindness toward Animals*. A comprehensive and extremely well-written survey from Genesis through 1990 by an advocate for the environment and animals. Regenstein's vision of environmentalism and animal protection as inextricably linked because they flow from the same spiritual source needs to be taken to heart by activists in both camps. The main emphasis is on Christianity, but there is a long chapter on Judaism and shorter chapters on Hinduism, Buddhism, Jainism, Islam, and Baha'i. Unfortunately—and undeservedly—out of print and hard to find.

Rosen, Steven, *Diet for Transcendence: Vegetarianism and the World Religions*. A brief but excellent survey of the attitude of several major religions, including Judaism and Christianity, toward vegetarianism and animal protection.

Schwartz, Richard H., Ph.D., *Judaism and Vegetarianism*. A comprehensive look at animal protection and vegetarianism from a Jewish perspective. A rare combination of scholarship and readability by a pioneering scholar and activist.

Webb, Stephen H., *On God and Dogs: A Christian Theology of Compassion for Animals*. Focusing on companion animals, and the personal relationships between humans and animals, Webb, a Protestant theologian, moves beyond the traditional Christian (i.e., Pauline) view while stopping short of adopting an animal rights position. The fact that it points in the right direction while not appearing too "radical" may make *On God and Dogs* a valuable bridge to the mainstream Christian community.

——. *Good Eating*. Webb commends vegetarianism and compassionate treatment of animals as expressions of Christian faith and stewardship. While I wish he were more sympathetic to animal rights, *Good Eating* will be an effective bridge to conservative Christian communities.

Young, Richard Alan, *Is God a Vegetarian? Christianity, Vegetarianism, and Animal Rights*. A professor of New Testament studies at Temple Baptist Seminary, Young takes a conservative approach to historical questions such as "Did Jesus eat meat?" but believes that historical questions are less important than spiritual ones, concluding that vegetarianism is not required by Christianity, but represents an ethical ideal to which all Christians should aspire. Although I wish Young were a little more "radical," this is one of the most informative books available on the Bible and animals.

Animal Rights

Achor, Amy Bount, *Animal Rights: A Beginner's Guide.* An excellent introduction to the issues of the animal protection movement. Nearly half the book's four hundred plus pages are devoted to a comprehensive resource guide. Important reading for anyone interested in becoming active on behalf of animals.

Fox, Michael W., *Inhumane Society: The American Way of Exploiting Animals.* Although in my view it does not go far enough (Dr. Fox seems to believe, for example, that there is such a thing as "humane" slaughter), this is nonetheless one of the best books available on the status and treatment of animals in America. By a veterinarian and vice-president of the Humane Society of the United States.

Francione, Gary, *Introduction to Animal Rights: Your Child or the Dog?* An accessible, comprehensive introduction to the theory and practical implications of animal rights by an attorney who is a leading proponent of legal rights for animals. The Appendix: "Twenty Questions (and Answers)" alone is worth the purchase price.

Patterson, Charles, *Eternal Treblinka: Our Treatment of Animals and the Holocaust.* A thoughtful examination of the common roots of animal exploitation and atrocities against humans.

Regan, Tom, *The Case for Animal Rights.* A challenging book, written in the language of academic philosophy, by a leading animal rights philosopher.

Singer, Peter, *Animal Liberation.* This is the best-seller that started the modern animal rights movement, and it remains an indispensable classic.

Spiegel, Marjorie, *The Dreaded Comparison: Human and Animal Slavery.* An eye-opening comparison of the practices of human slavery and animal exploitation—and of the arguments used to justify them.

Companion Animals

Brestrup, Craig, *Disposable Animals: Ending the Tragedy of Throwaway Pets.* An accessible, insightful analysis of the tragedy of our system of companion animal ownership and population control. Anyone reading it will understand why we must all begin to see ourselves as our companions' guardians rather than their owners.

Hunting

Amory, Cleveland, *Mankind? Our Incredible War on Wildlife.* Originally published in 1974, this is the classic exposé of hunting in America by the founder of The Fund for Animals and the best-selling author of *The Cat Who Came for Christmas* and *Ranch of Dreams.*

Baker, Ron, *The American Hunting Myth.* An informed and well-reasoned deconstruction of the arguments that the hunting industry uses to defend its bloodsport.

Vegan Lifestyle

Berry, Rynn, *Famous Vegetarians and their Favorite Recipes: Lives and Lore from Buddha to the Beatles.* Brief sketches of thirty-two famous vegetarians. Well researched and entertaining, by the history advisor to the North American Vegetarian Society.

Marcus, Erik, *Vegan: The New Ethics of Eating.* An excellent introduction to the ethical, ecological, social, and health reasons for adopting a vegan diet. Essential reading.

Moran, Victoria, *Compassion: The Ultimate Ethic, An Exploration of Veganism.* The classic "why to" and "how to" book on adopting a vegan lifestyle. As valuable now as when it was first published.

Stepaniak, Joanne, *The Vegan Sourcebook* and *Being Vegan: Living with Conscience, Conviction, and Compassion.* Between them, these two books will tell you everything you need to know about vegan living. Gentle and down to earth, these beautifully written books will take the anxiety out of changing your lifestyle.

Bibliography

Bibles

Analytical Greek New Testament, analysis by Barbara and Timothy Friberg, Baker Book House, Grand Rapids, MI, 1981.

The Holy Bible in the King James Version, Thomas Nelson Publishers, Nashville, TN, 1984.

The Holy Bible: The New Revised Standard Version, Oxford University Press, New York, 1977.

The Interlinear Greek-English New Testament with Lexicon and Synonyms, ed. George Ricker Berry, Zondervan Publishing House, Grand Rapids, MI, 1958.

The Interlinear NIV Hebrew-English Old Testament, edited by John R. Kohlenberger III, Zondervan Publishing House, Grand Rapids, MI, 1987.

Latin Vulgate, The Unbound Bible, World Wide Web site sponsored by Biola University, La Mirada, CA, http://unbound.biola.edu.

The New American Bible for Catholics, Greenlawn Press, South Bend, IN, 1991.

The New English Bible, Oxford University Press, Cambridge University Press, 1970.

The New Inductive Study Bible: The New American Standard Bible, Updated Edition, The Lockman Foundation, La Habra, CA, 1995, Precept Ministries International and Harvest House Publishers, Eugene, OR, 2000.

The NIV Study Bible, Kenneth Barker, General Editor, Zondervan Publishing House, Grand Rapids, MI, 1995.

The Septuagint with Apocrypha: Greek and English, edited and translated by Sir Lancelot C. L. Brenton, Hendrickson Publishers, 1986.

Tanakh: The Holy Scriptures, The Jewish Publication Society, Philadelphia, 1985.

Bible Study Aids

Brown, F., S. Driver and C. Briggs, *The Brown-Driver-Briggs Hebrew and English Lexicon,* Hendrickson Publishers, Inc., Peabody, MA, 1997.

Strong, James, LL.D., S.T.D., *The New Strong's Exhaustive Concordance of the Bible,* Thomas Nelson Publishers, Nashville, TN, 1996.

Tenney, Merrill C., general editor, *The Zondervan Pictorial Bible Dictionary,* Zondervan Publishing House, Grand Rapids, MI, 1967.

Thayer, Joseph Henry, *A Greek-English Lexicon of the New Testament,* Baker Book House, Grand Rapids, MI, 1977.

Verbrugge, Verlyn D., ed., *The NIV Theological Dictionary of New Testament Words,* Zondervan Publishing House, Grand Rapids, MI, 2000.

Vine, W. E., Merrill F. Unger, William White, Jr., *Vine's Complete Expository Dictionary of Old and New Testament Words,* Thomas Nelson Publishers, Nashville, TN, 1996.

Wigram, George V., *The Englishman's Greek Concordance of the New Testament,* Hendrickson Publishers, Peabody, MA, 1999.

——. *The Englishman's Hebrew Concordance of the Old Testament,* Hendrickson Publishers, Peabody, MA, 1999.

Zondervan NASB Exhaustive Concordance, Zondervan Publishing House, Grand Rapids, MI, 2000.

General

Achor, Amy Bount, *Animal Rights: A Beginner's Guide,* WriteWare Inc., Yellow Springs, OH, 1996.

Akers, Keith, *A Vegetarian Sourcebook: The Nutrition, Ecology, and Ethics of a Natural Foods Diet,* Vegetarian Press, Denver, 1989.

——. *The Lost Religion of Jesus: Simple Living and Nonviolence in Early Christianity,* Lantern Books, New York, 2000.

Amory, Cleveland, *Mankind: Our Incredible War on Wildlife*, Harper and Row, New York, 1974.

Aristotle, *Politics*, translated by Ernest Barker, Oxford University Press, Oxford, 1995.

Baker, Ron, *The American Hunting Myth*, Vantage Press, New York, 1985.

Barber, Theodore Xenophon, Ph.D., *The Human Nature of Birds: A Scientific Discovery with Startling Implications*, St. Martin's Press, New York, 1993.

Barnstone, Willis, ed., *The Other Bible: Jewish Pseudepigrapha, Christian Apocrypha, Gnostic Scriptures, Kabbalah, Dead Sea Scrolls, Edited with Introductions by Willis Barnstone*, HarperSanFrancisco, New York, 1984.

Bentham, Jeremy, *Introduction to the Principles of Morals and Legislation*, Hafner Press, New York, 1948.

Berry, Rynn, *Famous Vegetarians and Their Favorite Recipes: Lives and Lore from Buddha to the Beatles*, Pythagorean Publishers, New York, 1999.

——. *Food for the Gods: Vegetarianism and the World's Religions*, Pythagorean Publishers, New York, 1998.

Bekoff, Marc, ed., *The Smile of a Dolphin: Remarkable Accounts of Animal Emotions*, Discovery Books/Random House, New York, 2000.

Brestrup, Craig, *Disposable Animals: Ending the Tragedy of Throwaway Pets*, Camino Bay Books, Leander, TX, 1997.

Catechism of the Catholic Church with Modifications from the Editio Typica, Doubleday, New York, 1995.

Davis, Karen, Ph.D., *Prisoned Chickens, Poisoned Eggs: An Inside Look at the Modern Poultry Industry*, Book Publishing Company, Summertown, TN, 1996.

——. *More Than a Meal: The Turkey in History, Myth, Ritual, and Reality*, Lantern Books, New York, 2001.

Dostoyevsky, Fyodor, *The Brothers Karamazov*, translated by Constance Garnett, The Modern Library, Random House, New York, 1950.

Dunkerley, Roderic, *Beyond the Gospels: An Investigation into the Information on the Life of Christ to be Found Outside the Gospels*, Penguin Books, Hammondsworth, Middlesex, UK, 1957.

Durant, Will, *The Life of Greece*, Simon and Schuster, New York, 1939.

Eisenman, Robert, *James the Brother of Jesus: The Key to Unlocking the Secrets of Early Christianity and the Dead Sea Scrolls,* Viking, New York, 1997.

Eisnitz, Gail A., *Slaughterhouse: The Shocking Story of Greed, Neglect, and Inhumane Treatment Inside the U.S. Meat Industry,* Prometheus Books, Amherst, NY, 1997.

Eusebius, *The History of the Church from Christ to Constantine,* Penguin Books, Hammondsworth, UK, 1965.

Fouts, Roger, with Stephen Tukel Mills, *Next of Kin: My Conversations with Chimpanzees,* Avon Books, New York, 1997.

Fox, Dr. Michael W., *Inhumane Society: The American Way of Exploiting Animals,* St. Martin's Press, New York, 1990.

Free, Ann Cottrell, *Animals, Nature and Albert Schweitzer,* The Flying Fox Press, Washington, D.C., 1988.

Francione, Gary L., *Introduction to Animal Rights: Your Child or the Dog?* Temple University Press, Philadelphia, 2000.

Giehl, Dudley, *Vegetarianism: A Way of Life,* Harper and Row, New York, 1979.

Hornblower, Simon and Tony Spawforth, eds., *Who's Who in the Classical World,* Oxford University Press, Oxford, 2000.

Hyland, J. R., *God's Covenant With Animals: A Biblical Basis for the Humane Treatment of All Creatures,* Lantern Books, New York, 2000.

Kalechofsky, Roberta, Ph.D., ed., *Judaism and Animal Rights: Classical and Contemporary Responses,* Micah Publications, Marblehead, MA, 1992.

——. *Vegetarian Judaism: A Guide for Everyone,* Micah Publications, Marblehead, MA, 1998.

Kook, Abraham Isaac, *Abraham Isaac Kook: The Lights of Penitence, The Moral Principles, Lights of Holiness, Essays, Letters, and Poems,* Paulist Press, Mahwah, NJ, 1978.

Kowalski, Gary, *The Souls of Animals,* Stillpoint Publishing, Walpole, NH, 1991.

——. *The Bible According to Noah: Theology as if Animals Mattered,* Lantern Books, New York, 2001.

Kreisler, Kristin von, *The Compassion of Animals: True Stories of Animal Courage and Kindness*, Prima Publishing, Rocklin, CA, 1997.

———. *Beauty in the Beasts: True Stories of Animals Who Choose to Do Good*, Tarcher/Putnam, New York, 2001.

Linden, Eugene, *The Parrot's Lament and Other True Tales of Animal Intrigue, Intelligence, and Ingenuity*, Dutton, New York, 1999.

Linzey, Andrew, *Animal Gospel*, Westminster John Knox Press, Louisville, 2000.

———. *Animal Theology*, University of Illinois Press, Urbana, 1995.

———. *Christianity and the Rights of Animals*, Crossroad, New York, 1991.

Marcus, Erik, *Vegan: The New Ethics of Eating*, McBooks Press, Ithaca, NY, 1998.

Mason, Jim, and Peter Singer, *Animal Factories: What Agribusiness is Doing to the Family Farm, the Environment and Your Health*, Harmony Books, New York, 1990 (revised and updated).

Masson, Jeffrey Moussaieff and Susan McCarthy, *When Elephants Weep: The Emotional Lives of Animals*, Delacorte Press, New York, 1995.

Moran, Victoria, *Compassion, The Ultimate Ethic: An Exploration of Veganism*, Thorsons Publishers Limited, Wellingborough, UK, 1985.

Murti, Vasu, *"They Shall Not Hurt or Destroy": Moral and Theological Objections to the Human Exploitation of Animals*, Vasu Murti, Oakland, CA, undated.

Patterson, Charles, *Eternal Treblinka: Our Treatment of Animals and the Holocaust*, Lantern Books, New York, 2002.

Ponting, Clive, *A Green History of the World: The Environment and the Collapse of Great Civilizations*, St. Martin's Press, New York, 1991.

Randour, Mary Lou, Ph.D., *Animal Grace: Entering a Spiritual Relationship with Our Fellow Creatures*, New World Library, Novato, CA, 2000.

Regan, Tom, and Peter Singer, eds., *Animal Rights and Human Obligations*, Prentice Hall, Englewood Cliffs, NJ, 1989 (second edition).

Regan, Tom, *The Case for Animal Rights*, University of California Press, Berkeley, 1983.

Regenstein, Lewis G., *Replenish the Earth: A History of Organized Religion's Treatment of Animals and Nature—Including the Bible's Message of Conservation and Kindness Toward Animals*, Crossroad, New York, 1991.

Rosen, Steven, *Diet for Transcendence: Vegetarianism and the World's Religions*, Torchlight, Badger, CA, 1997.

Ryder, Richard D., *Animal Revolution: Changing Attitudes Toward Speciesism*, Basil Blackwell, Ltd., Oxford, UK, 1989.

——. *Victims of Science: The Use of Animals in Research*, National Anti-Vivisection Society Limited, London, 1983 (second and revised edition).

Schwartz, Richard, *Judaism and Vegetarianism* (New Revised Edition), Lantern Books, New York, 2001.

Singer, Isaac Bashevis, *The Collected Stories of Isaac Bashevis Singer,* The Noonday Press, New York, 1996.

Singer, Peter, *Animal Liberation*, New York Review/Random House, New York, 1990 (second and revised edition).

Spong, John Shelby, *Rescuing the Bible from Fundamentalism: A Bishop Rethinks the Meaning of Scripture*, HarperSanFrancisco, New York, 1991.

Stepaniak, Joanne, *The Vegan Sourcebook*, McGraw-Hill, New York, 2000.

——. *Being Vegan: Living with Conscience, Conviction, and Compassion*, Lowell House, Los Angeles, 2000.

Webb, Stephen H., *On God and Dogs: A Christian Theology of Compassion for Animals*, Oxford University Press, New York, 1998.

——. *Good Eating,* Brazos Press, Grand Rapids, MI, 2001.

Wesley, John, "The General Deliverance" in *Sermons of John Wesley* on the website of the General Board of Global Ministries of the United Methodist Church.

Wynne-Tyson, Jon, ed., *The Extended Circle: A Dictionary of Humane Thought*, Centaur Press, Fontwell Sussex, 1985.

Young, Richard Alan, *Is God a Vegetarian? Christianity, Vegetarianism, and Animal Rights*, Open Court, Peru, IL, 1999.

Of related interest from Lantern Books

Keith Akers
The Lost Religion of Jesus
Simple Living and Nonviolence in Early Christianity

Akers argues that Jewish Christianity was vegetarian and practiced pacifism and communal living. "A whole new conception of Christianity."—**Walter Wink**

Marc Bekoff
Strolling with Our Kin
Speaking for and Respecting Voiceless Animals
Foreword by Jane Goodall

"A philosophical and ethical odyssey that examines how we can all live in harmony with our kindred creatures."—*The Animals' Agenda*

Judy Carman
Peace To All Beings
Veggie Soup for the Chicken's Soul
Foreword by Gene Bauston

This is a guidebook full of miracle-making tools. Lighten up your journey with inspiration, meditations, heartfelt stories, over seventy prayers, and solid, fact-based reasons that explain why we human beings must make peace with the animal nations if we are ever to find true inner peace, heal our earth, and create authentic world peace.

Carol Adams
The Inner Art Trilogy
Spiritual Practices for Body and Soul

The Inner Art of Vegetarianism

In language that is gentle and graceful, Carol Adams shows us how to be more effective in easing the suffering of others by engaging our own, and how to better cope with our own suffering by engaging the suffering of animals.

" 'Together,' she tells us, 'vegetarianism and spiritual practice say, "I will not be violent to myself or others. I cultivate nonviolence within myself because I see myself connected to others.' "—*Satya*

The Inner Art of Vegetarianism Workbook

For those who wish to enhance their own spirituality or vegetarianism, the *Workbook* provides a way to begin or continue the spiritual practices introduced in *The Inner Art of Vegetarianism*.

"True to her heart, Carol Adams boldly continues the fight against prejudice in general and one form of prejudice in particular. It is a prejudice so deeply rooted and ingrained in us that we hardly notice. It is our prejudice against animals."—**Sharon Gannon**, Jivamukti Yoga™ Center

Meditations on The Inner Art of Vegetarianism

Adams provides daily inspiring guidance to anyone who is or wants to become a vegetarian. Each day comes with a reflection, a brief elucidation, and a practice—all three setting in motion the possibility of transformation. Invaluable for all those who are beginning on the path of compassion, health, conscious living, and peaceful eating.

J. R. Hyland
God's Covenant with Animals
A Biblical Basis for the Humane Treatment of All Creatures

The Bible, argues Hyland, calls upon human beings to stop their violence and abuse of each other and other creatures. "A daring and profoundly original work . . ."—**Stephen H. Webb**, author, *On God and Dogs*

Gary Kowalski
The Bible According to Noah
Theology as If Animals Mattered

Kowalski explores the ancient stories of the Bible to examine their relevance today—especially in regard to how we view and treat other animals.

Martin Rowe, Editor
The Way of Compassion
Vegetarianism, Environmentalism, Animal Advocacy, and Social Justice
A Stealth Technologies Book

"Sophisticated but not inaccessible, this . . . important and deeply engaging book belongs in all but the smallest libraries."—*Library Journal*

Richard H. Schwartz, Ph.D.
Judaism and Global Survival

"A shofar calling the Jewish community to wake up to current crises and at the same time return to our roots."
—**Mark X. Jacobs**

Richard H. Schwartz, Ph.D.
Judaism and Vegetarianism
New Revised Edition

"Schwartz has made a case that is difficult to refute, in a book you will find difficult to ignore."—*Jerusalem Post*
"Fully documented and very convincing . . . A well-done treatise on a subject of increasing interest."—*Library Journal*

At your bookstore or from the publisher:
Lantern Books
1 Union Square West Suite 201
New York, NY 10003
212-414-2275
www.lanternbooks.com